365 Ways to POWER UP YOUR LIFE:

Tools for Intuitive Living

By Lilly White

Love Your Life Publishing
Wilmington, DE
www.loveyourlifepublishing.com
ISBN: 978-1-934509-88-3

Cover design by 2FacedDesign.com
Editing by Gwen Hoffnagle
Author photos by Shawn De Salvo

Advance Praise for 365 Ways to Power Up Your Life

"This book is not only inspired, it's a valuable life tool. I highly recommend adding this treasure to your bookshelf."
~ Caroline Myss, author of *Sacred Contracts* and *Anatomy of the Spirit*

"Lilly's wisdom and inspiration shine out of these pages. She knows grief all to intimately but has not allowed it to define her. Instead she uses her experiences to show her readers how to be each day with grief in all its stages. These bite-sized nuggets can be easily read and practiced each day. This is truly a powerful book on how to get through grief graciously."
~ Anne DeButte, Heartbreak to Happiness® coach and author of *Grief's Abyss: Finding Your Pathway to Peace*

"This book will bring a smile to you every day as Lilly's magical spirit, playfulness and wisdom come through the entire book. It will both lift your spirit and inspire your mind."
~ Ramila Padiachy, D.N.M®, R.Ac

"Very insightful! Very powerful! Gentle daily reminders of the beauty, gifts and miracles that surround our lives if we just take a moment to discover and acknowledge them."
~ Dr. Michaela Cadeau, Doctor of Chiropractic

Dedicated to John, my husband of over forty years

And the spirit of marriage

Table of Contents

Introduction

The book you hold in your hands was birthed through death. It took three years – a long birth. The paradox is that loss and death surrounded me before I finally gave birth to *365 Ways to Power Up Your Life: Tools for Intuitive Living* and the pages of "Let Spirit have you."

It began on May 30th, 2012, at 3:33, when two police officers came to our door and told me our daughter of thirty-seven years had taken her life. Melanie lived away from us, and this was the only way for her to reach John and me. I fell to my knees and asked the question "Is this what forgiveness looks like?" You will read more about that day in Day 232 below.

It was a Wednesday, and the previous Monday my mom, Rosemary, was diagnosed with colon cancer. The Holy Mother has risen. The organism of life is having its way with me. It is breathtaking, but I am breathing; surviving, but barely. I am on my knees daily praying to Holy Mother and the God of my understanding as Saint Teresa of Avila did so many centuries ago. I am giving myself daily to a power greater than myself. It is the only way I can survive.

Three months later my dad had a stroke. He was on the same ward in the hospital in Calgary, Alberta, as my mother. John and I live in Almonte, just outside of Ottawa, Ontario, a four-hour flight from Calgary.

I had opened a business, the White Lilly, in 2011. Due to the context of the following year, I was not at the store as much as I would like to have been. The grief was like waves washing over me daily, the ocean drowning me as I continued to swim as fast as I could to reach the shore of reality.

The travelling back and forth to visit Mom and Dad took its toll on my body. There was a price to pay. I broke out in shingles twice in 2013. (Shingles is a viral infection that causes a painful rash.)

By October of 2013, Mom had passed, Dad was in a care home, and my business had crumbled. We had been debt-free when I opened the business, but now we were in debt for well over $150,000. I was tired and numb, but I continued to "let Spirit have me."

In those three years I lost friends and family members, not through death but through the transformation of defeat. They did not understand my loss or my anger.

I continue to pray; it's all I have. Most days it's all I believe in. I certainly do not believe in myself. I am empty. I am in a dark night of the soul. But I am fortunate to understand that this is necessary, and I continue to pray and play every day. H.O.P.E. for me is Helping Others Pray/Play Everyway.

My prayer – my hope for you as you read these daily prayers – is that you learn to hand yourself over to something bigger than yourself – a power greater than an authority over you:

an empowered spirit within you. That energy comes from another source, and when you pray it becomes you.

This book is an antidote for all your woes and troubles. When we love big, we grieve deeply, and that is our gift – to have loved and been loved.

Just for today... let the Spirit of LOVE have you.

What Does "Power Up Your Life" Mean?

It is a name that my husband suggested when I was trying to find a title for a weekend retreat. I wanted a name that would attract both males and females. He asked me, "What is the purpose of the weekend?" I responded, "That people come away with tools; that they feel empowered." As I answered, I had a vision of a tool box, of power tools... So Power Up Your Life came into being. That was in 2009, and it has been a work in progress, with YOU in mind.

How do you Power Up Your Life when all seems lost? When people around you are dying... lying... hiding?

How do you live in harmony and address the community when our society is about to blow up with control and fear?

My wish for you as you read these daily inspirations is that you take these poems — these daily affirmations — as tools to enrich your life. May you see yourself... your spirit. Some are written from a child's perspective, some from the wisdom of Goddess, some from the ethers of the unknown.

Thank you, John, my knight of forty years, for leaving me alone when I was in the spirit world.

Thank you, Amanda, for loving me unconditionally.

Our grandchildren — thank you for your trust and love.

Melanie, thank you for being beside me, always in all ways.

Thank you, Elaine Luedey, for believing in me.

Thank you, Cyrilla, for allowing me to question everything.

Thank you, Diana; you are always there with non-judgment.

Thank you, Jill Angelo Birnbaum, with gratitude for your faith in me, your love of my madness and your fairy wisdom.

Thanks also to Rona Fraser and Lynn Mayer for all your help and patience. I also send thanks to Rondi Brown for your belief and starting me on my way hosting Angel workshops, "Calling all Angles," so very long ago. You are the Wise One with angel wings.

Thank you, Caroline Myss and Andrew Harvey, with the deepest of gratitude for everything. Caroline, I love you in the deepest way, not only for your work but for all you give of yourself.

We are all powerful human beings but sometimes we allow ourselves to get caught up in the chaos of everyday living. How do we Power Up Our Lives and stay focused? It is easy if we allow ourselves to "Let Spirit Have Us." What does that mean? Let go; let God. Surrender to each moment. My hope as you read through these 365 Ways to POWER UP YOUR LIFE is that you come to realize that you are an empowered human being. You have all the tools you need to live a congruent life, a joy-filled life, a life worth living. May these simple tools help you on your journey.

I have written these simple tools with Saint Theresa of Avila in mind. I was introduced to her through my studies with Caroline Myss. When I met Caroline, she was writing her book *Entering the Castle* based on the works of Saint Theresa of Avila. I was smitten with the statue of Saint Theresa by Bernini. Theresa is taken over by spirit in what can only be described as giving herself completely, similar to the orgasm of our bodies when we release. She is in total release to spirit. So I decided to write daily inspirations called "Just for today, let Spirit have you," hence this pocketbook. My hope is that you release yourself of EGO (Edging God Out) and allow Spirit to have you. When this happens you are in the flow of life, in the spirit of who YOU are.

To support you in your journey and help you implement the ideas in this book, I've created the *Power Up Your Life 30-Day Challenge Workbook*. It's my free gift to you. You can download it at www.lillywhite.ca

DAY 1

Happy New Year!

Happy New Year, one and all!

May this year bring you an abundance of Joy, Peace, Hope, Compassion, Unity and Love.

Today and always, let Spirit have you.

This year, make your life happen; make your life shine. May you know the bright being of light that you are.

Just for today...

...let the Spirit of Happy New Year have you.

DAY 2

The Spirit of a New Year

May this new year bring you an abundance of Joy, Peace, Hope, Compassion, Unity and Love.

Start a list today. What do you love today? What is not making you happy?

How can you change? Do you need to change? How about making yourself an altar; your very own Sacred Space? This altar will alter your consciousness as you go into the new year.

Congratulations, you have made it this far.

Do not take it lightly; you are here for a reason. This year you are about to discover the reason.

Just for today...

... let the Spirit of the New Year and New Beginnings have you.

DAY 3

The Spirit of Melanie

A friend, Patricia, asked a question: "What do you think happens to us after we take our last breath; do you believe we come back?"

I forget my answer at the time, but have come to a knowing about it. When we were in Bali in November of 2013, I attended a channelling session with a priest (such a session is a must when visiting beloved Bali). I always leave my body and go into the ethers in such situations. At this session, John, my husband of forty years, sat in the back. I was up front, and our daughter Melanie came through. The energy smelled like her, sounded like her, and felt like her. I rocked her as she wept, saying she was sorry, and she gave me messages for each of her children. I continued to rock until her weeping stopped. Then she said, "I am leaving now; I am going into the stars." At the time I did not understand, but the session left both John and me feeling that she was okay, and we were as if in a semi-trance for almost three days.

I am sure you have experienced this bliss in meditation from time to time. On the flight home I watched *Winter's Tale* with

Colin Farrell. It relates to our becoming stars. After the movie I slept, went into the in-between sleep states, and just knew I had our answer: For those of us who die at lower energy or frequency and are still working on "How do I best serve?" as opposed to "What do I deserve?" our energy goes back into the collective and is reborn. Those who die at faster frequency go towards the inner universe and become stars.

Sometimes we need the help, as Melanie did. All was forgiven and she was released.

Just for today...

... let the Spirit of the Ethers have you.

DAY 4

The Spirit of Death or Rebirth

When we die, we go back into the collective. There is no judgment — neither in light nor shadow — only observations. We come into this lifetime with free will and a sacred contract, so the collective does not want anything or require anything from us. Suffering is part of the human experience, and what brings one person to suffer may not affect another; it depends on their sacred contract. Our loved ones observe and we must ask for their assistance. This assistance is not something tangible; it comes in the form of peace, hope, love, joy, and forgiveness. These are all we ever really need — these and acceptance.

With these tools we can move mountains, help where needed and serve the universe with grace and prayer.

Just for today...

... let the Spirit of Living Now have you.

DAY 5

The Spirit of Gratitude

I am grateful
my heart does not hurt like before
my feet can tap and dance on the floor

I am grateful
for the peace in my heart
to KNOW that my loved ones
who have transitioned
we are never apart

I am grateful
this season is coming to an end
for in its changing
we begin again

I am grateful
to those who are with me still
the air that we breathe
to love, pray and play
the adventure, the thrill

I am grateful
I am spirit, my soul alive
Thank you, God/Goddess
I flourish, I thrive

Just for today…

… let the Spirit of Gratitude have you.

DAY 6

The Spirit of the Magic

Today we celebrate the Epiphany.

I am enjoying gifts from three wise friends.
One gave the gift of compassion,
One, wisdom,
The other, relaxation.
Gifts rich with golden nuggets for the mind, body and soul.
Sometimes gifts come in the least expected spaces and places.

Just for today…

… let the gifts of the Magi have you.

DAY 7

The Spirit of Your Cage

Baby, you're already in a cage and it is not locked. It's your thoughts, your self-doubt, your clutter, your wants and your desires. Your inability to forgive, your grief, your "I don't give a shit what day it is." Your judgments, your pettiness, your cleverness, your shrewdness.

Get over yourself. Life is for living — not longing or wanting.

It's for feeling, forgiveness and fun. It's for playfulness and praying.

Hey, I'm just saying: Here is your key — get out of your head and into your heart, your cage is ready to fall apart. It does not hold you, you are free. Get out, get out.

You are spirit; just be. Just BE.

Just for today…

… let the Spirit of Release have you.

DAY 8

The Spirit of the Sun

As the sun rises this morning, bow in prayer.

"Beloved Sun, do you have a secret?"

"Yes," replies the sun. "I am the sum of the parts of you that you have not owned. I am the fire that burns within you. I am the father to your soul. I am the power of your creation.
I am not a separate being, as none of you are, but I am a conscious conduit of ultimate light and energy.
Together we are divine consciousness.
Embrace me this day. Fill your eyes with my light, that you may share with others."

"Thank you, Beloved Sun."

Just for today…

… let the Spirit of the Sun have you.

DAY 9

The Spirit of Grief

This day can also be called "The Spirit of Body Talk."

Are you suffering from any infection this week?
All is in GOD (Good Orderly Direction) when we are aware of the energy involved.

The body is a beautiful instrument from the Divine. It has its own song to sing when it's ready. It will talk to you, and show you what you are working on.

If you are feeling ill — embrace, release.

Just for today...

... let the Spirit of Your Body talk to you.

DAY 10

The Spirit of Our Senses

"Hear that?" asked God/Goddess.

— Yes. It is the sound of a peaceful twilight.

See that?

— Yes. It is the setting of a day's end.

Smell that?

— Yes. It is the apples in their decay, lying under the tree for one more day.

Feel that?

— Yes. It is the pulse of life kicking in anticipation of a journey into life.

Ah, you have paid attention to the details today.

— Yes.

Just for today...

... let the Spirit of Life have you.

DAY 11

The Spirit of Anger

Anger is the God-given emotion that allows you to know a boundary has been violated.

Being aware is your first step.

The second step is doing something about it.

There is no need to lash out; feel the emotion, then allow the other to know how you feel.

You can do this with grace and love.

Just for today...

... let the Spirit of Your Boundaries have you.

DAY 12

The Spirit of Timelessness

Enjoy the moments, not the time involved in the moments, and the memories of those moments will last you a lifetime.

Just for today...

... let the Spirit of Timelessness have you.

DAY 13

The Spirit of Troubles

I have been asked, "How do you still shine, smile and laugh after the year you just experienced with the death of both your daughter and your mother?"

My response: "I am in grief; I am not in mourning. I am experiencing good grief. I believe the soul lives — in, around and through us. My child and my mother continue to grow and glow. If I continue to let Spirit have me, that means all of me — my mind, heart and soul. I am nearing my sixties and, if I live to be eighty, I only have another twenty Christmas trees, so I'd better get on with living and loving it!"

Just for today...

... give all your troubles away and let Spirit have you.

DAY 14

The Spirit of Goodbye

Are we ever really prepared for our last goodbye?

Are we ever really ready to let go? We wonder, "Why?"

Are we ever really conscious of the breaths
we take each day?

Are we able to nurture another as they breathe
their life away?

Can we sit in peaceful silence as they prepare to
leave in grace?

Can we hold their hand lightly when they meet their
maker face to face?

I will not wonder long as I travel once again to be at a loved
one's deathbed as she meets her final end.

In this ending begins a new journey that
only she will know,

But it won't be long before I meet her; a place of beauty she
will show.

We will come to understand we prepared for this long ago.

Spirit never dies; we change form, we burn in the hearts of loved ones as we continue to glow.

Just for today...

... let the Spirit of Goodbye have you.

DAY 15

The Spirit of Aging

I don't mind aging. What bothers me is that I feel I am changing from a fairy to a gnome. My nose is getting wider, my ears longer and my feet fatter.

Instead of growing up, I am growing out.

It is time to not take ourselves so seriously.
Laugh at our beauty.

Oh dear, I cannot say "This too shall pass," but I can say:

Just for today…

… let the Spirit of Aging have you.

DAY 16

The Spirit of Friendship

We have many friends.

We have spiritual friends,

Facebook friends, new friends,

Old friends, friendly friends...

But are we able to be good friends to ourselves?

Watch your thoughts today.

Praise yourself. See the light in yourself.

What you consider defects are usually what draw people to you.

Just for today...

... let the Spirit of True Friendship have you; be a friend to self.

DAY 17

The Spirit of Gut Feelings

Your gut has a brain.

It is a well-known fact that we have a brain in our gut – our "brain belly." In Michael Gershon's *The Second Brain* (Harper Collins), he says, "The second brain contains some 100 million neurons, more than in either the spinal cord or the peripheral nervous system."

Have you ever had butterflies in your stomach? Have you ever had that undeniable feeling in the pit of your stomach about someone or something? You don't say "I had a feeling in my finger" or "I had a feeling in my big toe." You say, "I feel it in my gut."

Sometimes we feel sick when we "know" something in our gut but do not act accordingly. We might even tell ourselves, "Listen to your heart." That kind of listening takes time; your stomach alerts you faster.

Feel what your gut is telling you today. Go with your instincts. Then your heart will say, "Well done."

Just for today...

...let the Spirit of Your Second Brain have you.

DAY 18

The Spirit of Your Heart

Follow your heart, breathe with your heart, live in your heart, love your heart open.

Here you will find your gift.

Just for today…

… let the Spirit of Your Open Heart have you.

If you have not downloaded your free gift, my newest workbook, *Power Up Your Life 30-Day Challenge Workbook*, waits for you at www.lillywhite.ca

DAY 19

The Spirit of Choices

I have seen the sun, seen the rain

I have felt the joy and felt the pain

I have heard the song, danced the dream

I have smelled my newborn; in her death, I did scream

I have touched reality, sensed the Divine

I have come to realize there is no Time

I must live my life, the choices are MINE.

Just for today…

… let the Spirit of Your Choices have you.

DAY 20

The Spirit of Exercise

The Divine, our prayers, cannot flow through us if we are holding tension.

Just for today, breathe, dance, do yoga, go to the gym, walk. These will help release stress or tension from your body. Allow your athletic self to shine through.

Just for today...

... let the Spirit of Exercise have you.

DAY 21

The Ticker List

Do you have a Ticker List?

That list of "to dos" before you are no more?

Time is not real; we invent time to handle our lives day to day.

One of the many things on my Ticker List was to dance with Jully Black, a Canadian songwriter/musician. It happened, on November 23rd, 2013. The beat of my heart with the beat of her rhythm.

Start your own Ticker List. It can be as simple as:

1. bake a cake of my own ingredients using my imagination
2. travel on my own, across oceans, the next village or across the city
3. take a dance class
4. play the cello
5. sleep for a full twelve hours
6. be brave in chaos

You get the idea. Your Ticker List can be anything you can imagine. Now go DO it!

Just for today…

… let the Spirit of a Ticker List have you.

DAY 22

The Spirit of Generosity

Do something special for someone today.

Only you and the Divine have any knowledge of what you are doing or giving.

Give freely with no expectations.

Just for today...

... let the Spirit of Generosity have you.

DAY 23

The Spirit of Your Journey

You do not have to keep running faster to reach your destination.

Slow and steady on the wings of the Divine — there you will reach your Destiny.

Slow Breath, Patience, Acceptance, Forgiveness — these are the only tools you need to pack.

Just for today…

… enjoy the Spirit of Your Personal Journey.

DAY 24

The Spirit of Om

The Rhythm

Mmmm, ahhhhh, nooooo, and okkkkk all add up to the eternal Ommmm.

This is the sound of our daughter Amanda giving birth in 2013; a highlight in my life.

I delivered two children by Cesarean section thirty-eight years ago, so I was fast asleep during their delivery. I was not around to witness our daughter Melanie giving birth, although I heard she was in sync, a beautiful hymn, a rhythm, the eternal Om. This same sound came from me when I found out about Melanie's death in May of 2012. I also heard this sound coming out of my mother
when she passed.

Watching Amanda give birth and holding space for her was hypnotic. There was a song emerging from her, a low hum that would rise up and then slow down. Finally, at the moment of Zofia's birth, there was a second of fear followed by Ommmm.

Spending time with Amanda and her family allowed me more time with Tatiana, Zofia's sister, who was two years old. I paid attention to Tatiana's rhythms and allowed her to be in them.

"I am hungry," she would say.

Or "I am full," "I don't want to," "I am ready now." Her need to cuddle. Her need to be alone in her imagination. Her endless love of the colour pink for her clothes. And her desire to run around naked. She is constantly in balance and rhythm.

Tatiana had the tummy of a two-year-old. She, and only she, knew when she was full. An hour later she was hungry. When I was raising my children, because I was the adult, I thought I knew their needs. I rushed them, angered them, and tantrums arose. I called it the terrible twos; now I understand it was a two-year-old fighting for her boundaries, her balance.

Patience is a gift, and although my time is still full when I am with Tatiana, I stop and allow the moments to flow and be in rhythm.

I understand why in Asian countries the grandparents often raise their children's children. Grandparents are not so busy making a living and rushing their kids out the door. We have the nerve to ask, "Why are kids these days on some type of drug to slow them down?" when it is us who have been speeding them up.

We live in a culture of accumulating stuff — mortgages, cars, wealth. Our children are our most valuable assets; they are the spirit of our tomorrows. If we want them to make good decisions for themselves, to be healthy citizens in our society, to be loving and responsible and to develop self–esteem, then we must do our part.

Slow down. Hear your Om.

Take a day off today and be with your child. Not on your rules, but on theirs. Just for this day. They have much to teach you. They will show you how to stop and listen, how to know when you are hungry, when to go for a nap, when to play, when to pray, when to cry, laugh and dance.

You will lose yourself in your own Ommmm.

Just for today...

...let the Spirit of Om have you.

DAY 25

The Spirit of Divine Channelling

We all have the ability to channel the Divine.

It can be through yoga, meditation, walking or breathing in the eternal Om, to name a few.

Good self-esteem is one of the tools that allow you to trust what you are hearing, seeing, witnessing. Asking "Is this really the Divine?" is EGO. First hit, best hit, I always say. Allow it to come in, pray the energy through, then let go.

It is part of our DNA to access the other side.
Believe, live, be.

Just for today...

...let the Spirit of Divine Channelling have you.

DAY 26

The Spirit of Praying

I am praying, playing, swaying,

At moments standing still.

Time has no reason or even a season

For moments when body does chill.

Simplicity is BEING, simply BREATHING the art of Spirit's will.

You discover that LIFE IS and can be a THRILL.

When you do, the whole of you, your energy, is free.

YOU, ME, WE become THEE.

Just for today…

… let the Spirit of Prayer have you.

DAY 27

The Spirit of Challenges

Don't Give Up. Let the spirit of your challenges have you.

Challenge has many forms; it all depends on who you are. What I consider a challenge, a block, may be an exercise for you.

When you allow yourself to understand, to feel that all is in divine order, the challenge becomes a blessing, a summons to discover your strength.

Just for today...

... let the Spirit of Challenges have you.

DAY 28

The Spirit of Grief

Just when you think that you have cried an ocean, a new wave comes up to greet you. You can either embrace it or push it away. I say, embrace it.

Grief comes in many forms: financial loss; loss of our good health; loss of a spouse, a child, a parent. Grief can be a loss of how we were, a shedding of our old self.

Whatever your grief is, ride the wave. Grief shows us the depth, the compassion of our love.

Just for today…

… let the Spirit of Good Grief have you.

DAY 29

Live Your Best Life

The day after I returned from my mother's funeral, we picked up Tatiana, our three-year-old granddaughter. Playing with her and living in the moment is precious, and allowed more grief to flow.

Upon awakening the next morning, this is what I heard my mother tell me:

Lilly, honour those who have gone home before you.

Live your BEST each and every day.

Help others in small, useful ways.

Do not be afraid to ask people if they need your help. Some may refuse, and that is okay.

Be kind to those who are angry.

Be angry when a boundary has been crossed, but not in a hurtful way.

Acknowledge and let go.

Stop trying to control the details.

And last but not least, continue to play and pray with your grandchildren, for yes, they are indeed the spirit of our tomorrows.

Love you, Your Mom

Just for today...

... let the Spirit of Living Your Best have you.

DAY 30

The Spirit of GOD

God, I love how you love me
I love when you show me things

When I am not looking
The skies, in the kitchen window

When I am joyfully cooking
I love when you direct me

When I am lost
You turn me around
Cause me to pause

I love how you heal me
When I'm rather sick

How you dance with me
When my step is too quick

I love when you hear me
When I am deaf

You bring a sparrow to perch
Slightly to my left

I love when I'm frightened
Unable to breathe

You do it for me
You breathe through me with ease

When I feel useless, unable to cope
Your daily reminder
Yes, I am Sister Hope.

Just for today…

… let the Spirit of God have you.

DAY 31

The Spirit of Pray and Play

When Spirit does say, "I am with you today"
My ears become alert. I hear the whisper
"Seek and serve — you've nothing to fear, it will not hurt,
Gather your resources I willingly gave, so you can share."

"It's your Karma," I say
When Spirit does say, "It's been a long day."

The moments were yours to live,
Your intent was clear, you were willing to hear
That alone you would not succeed,
That community is needed, the thoughts have
been seeded
To pray and play as a group, for this is the
way to understand.

That love is at your root.
When Spirit does say, "It is time to Pray."

I realize my mind has wandered.
I am into details, lists and consumption
Of things that pass away.
I take a deep breath, into my heart I melt.
Ah, "Here you are, God," your essence is felt.

When Spirit does say, "Seize this day," it is yours to Pray and Play.

Just for today...

...let the Spirit of Praying and Playing have you.

DAY 32

The Wisdom of Our Youth

Thank God for our youth, "the spirit of our tomorrows."

I once saw, on the news, a young man about ten years old. The interview was about what he thought of athletes injecting themselves with a substance in order to enhance their performance.

This young lad's answer: "IT DOES NOT MAKE SENSE, BE REAL, EITHER YOU HAVE IT IN YOU OR YOU DON'T!"

Just for today…

… let the Spirit of Your Tomorrows have you; listen to their wisdom.

DAY 33

When in Doubt

When in Doubt, do not shout, find out.

Sometimes our ego takes over and we are in fear that when we ask, someone we will be humiliated.

Humility is a gift of wisdom given to us through grace.

Just for today...

... let the Spirit of Your Doubts have you, release the fear to ASK;
you will be guided when you least expect it.

DAY 34

The Spirit of Gratitude

Live in the moment; stay in gratitude for the now.
Focus on what you have and who you are now.
Know that what you have is not who you are.
You are ENOUGH.

Do not postpone your happiness. Do not postpone your sadness. Embrace what is coming up now. Drugging, drinking, any addictive behaviour does not change things; it only makes you feel worse.

Write down three things you are grateful for today. They need not be people, places or things. They can be your health, your inner peace, your beautiful eyes, your ability to be creative in some small way.

We have a tendency to be grateful for people or things. What happens when your cat dies or your house burns down? I remember when I heard about the home that we were to purchase catching fire when our other home had been sold. Hmm... now I am free. That was my gratitude until we rebuilt.

Just for today...

... let the Spirit of Gratitude have you.

DAY 35

The Spirit of Your Creativity

Be creative.

Spirit rises up within you each day. Actually, spirit rises without you. You only have to be aware. Each breath is a creative state of grace. Ask yourself, "What am I creating today?"

It could be as simple as peeling potatoes, baking a cake, making a good cup of tea or running a tea company. You are a co-creator with the universe — now go create.

Just for today...

... let the Spirit of Your Creativity have you.

DAY 36

The Spirit of Your Business

Stay out of people's minds. What they think of you is none of your business. It is trespassing.

Will they like me? Am I good enough for them? What will they think?

Trying to change the way people think of you is like trying to raise the dead. It is not going to happen. They have their projections and those are usually about themselves. Let go; let God. Be yourself — the rest will happen, and you can rest.

You are loveable — that is all you need to know.

Just for today...

... let the Spirit of Minding Your Own Business have you.

DAY 37

The Spirit of Being a Volunteer

Be a volunteer.

Getting out of your head and into your body is a powerful force. Put that force into action. Step up. Who needs help in the community?

I've long said that we need "Communion within our Community"; breaking bread together.

Who can you be a companion to? Someone in a shop who needs flyers distributed, your local chamber of commerce, downtown committees, hospitals, shelters, pet stores... You get the idea.

Volunteering opens the volume of your heart.

Just for today...

... let the Spirit of Volunteering have you.

DAY 38

The Spirit of Your Breath

Breathe. Exercise. Play.

I studied yoga with Doreen Virtue and Caroline Myss, who bring in the best, and I still love my Kundalini yoga instructor, Suzanne Winlove-Smith, who is one of the best I have ever studied with. She continues to teach me about breathing and why it is so important.

Walk, don't run — you will still get where you need to go. Consciously walk, one step, breathe, another step… sing while you breathe, another step, laugh at how you feel… enjoy the walk, be it morning, noon or evening.

Play. Have you ever been to a party with a group of forty-somethings and played with squirt guns? It's fantastic.

I have been with children and painted by using a straw to blow the paint on the paper. It is pure play and the joy is unforgettable; the power within awakens the neglected child.

Just for today…

… let the Spirit of Breath, Exercise and Play have you.

DAY 39

The Spirit of Your Silent Witness

Do your best to get out of your own way today.
Become your silent witness.

If you make a mistake today, so what! Witness your reaction, take notes and, if you are upset by it, make a mental choice to change that behaviour.

Watch your thoughts when you are helping someone — what is your true intent?

When you are upset, what and who are you really upset with — yourself?

Trust me — once you know yourself, your inner witness will guide you.

Just for today...

... let the Spirit of Your Silent Witness have you.

DAY 40

The Spirit of Speaking with Kindness

To speak ill of someone,

even if you are upset,

is like taking a bad pill that gets stuck in your throat:

eventually, it will make YOU sick.

Just for today…

… let the Spirit of Speaking Words of Kindness and Compassion have you.

DAY 41

The Spirit of Obsession

Do not obsess.

This is easier said than done.

When you have a thought, filter it through, breathe it, visualize the thought being grounded and... LET GO.

I suggest a simple visualization to my clients: See the thought go through your body, into the soles of your feet, into the soul of the earth. The thought will awaken when your soul is ready to do what needs to be done, and your witness will guide you.

Just for today...

... let the Spirit of Letting Go of Obsessing have you.

DAY 42

The Spirit of Your Smile

Smile.

It's easier than frowning, which requires seventy-eight muscles. A smile uses only fourteen.

Look in the mirror and try it. See — no one is looking, only your divine self.

Smile when driving to work, when picking up groceries or doing your chores around the house. Smile at the postman, the paperboy. Smile when you are talking to friends, either on the phone or on Facebook. Smile when praying, playing. Smile, and the whole world smiles back. You never know whom your smile will heal today.

Just for today...

... let the Spirit of Your Smile heal someone today.

DAY 43

The Spirit of Expecting the Best

Expect the best, not the worst, of both people and situations.

Old behaviour, old patterns — yes, they come back and we can get stuck in them. Just for today, see the best in yourself, others and any situation that comes up.

When we are in the habit of expecting the best, when darkness appears we do not dwell on it as we are still expecting the BEST.

Just for today...

... let the Spirit of Your Best have you.

DAY 44

The Spirit of Prayer

Infuse me with thy grace,
On this day, my labour I face.

Infuse me with thy peace,
On this day, I help erase suffering with ease.

Infuse me with thy flame,
On this day, I accept, not blame.

Infuse me with thy kindness,
On this day, I see without blindness.

Infuse me with thy gentleness,
On this day, I observe, I witness.

Infuse me with thy love, Lord,
On this day, I feel compassion
And put it into action.

Just for today...

... let the Spirit of Prayer have you.

DAY 45

The Spirit of Archetypes

Step into the wheel that starts with who you are;
As you move through your houses you'll reach
your farthest star.
You'll understand your motives for getting up each day.
You'll realize you have chosen to live your life your way.

Eventually you'll discover you knew it all along;
You'll be guided to the light side of what you thought was
right from wrong.
You may think you're a damsel who lives in
much distress—
You do not need a knight; your life was just a test.

Maybe it was courage you thought that you had lacked;
Your bully was in the light when you felt attacked.
The study of your journey, of going deep within
Is what this workshop brings you, so now we will begin

To unravel all your mysteries you did put into place;
You are ready to hold the mirror and see that
you are grace.
Your highest potential beckons; come within your wheel.
The pathway to your soul is how your life will heal.

Just for today...

... let the Spirit of Your Archetypes guide you;
find out all you can about yourself.

DAY 46

The Spirit of Angels

Calling all angels
I sit here to write
A message to receive
I am filled with delight

Hearing your message
Being still in the now
Perhaps I will feel you
Or sense you somehow

The essence of you
I am willing to know
What my life plan is
I'm hoping you'll show

Calling all angels
It is flowing within
Onto this paper
Now I begin

To unravel the pieces
I put into place
With your sweet essence
I am now filled with grace

Just for today...

... let the Spirit of Your Angels have you.

DAY 47

The Spirit of Your Dreams

Entering into the nightlight of my soul
I release my ego
Of images untold
Into the depths of energies

I cannot see
I review myself
To the space
Here we become thee
I see, I feel, I hear
The images of the unknown

Upon awakening
I realize that in dreaming
I am home

Just for today…

… let the Spirit of Your Dreams have you.

DAY 48

The Spirit of Ego

Become aware when you are in EGO.

EGO = Edging God Out.

As soon as you become aware that something is about you, ask why and what is your intent behind your self-saboteur.

Example: you lose your job. YOU are not your job — it is a means to an end, a way to pay the mortgage, feed yourself and family, etc. Do not take it personally by asking, "What is the matter with me?" Ask instead, "What is the meaning in this situation?" Ask for guidance from a friend, mentor or elder.

Just for today…

… let the Spirit of Letting Go of EGO have you.

DAY 49

Fairies DO Exist: A Fairy Story

In January of 2001, my husband, John, was posted to Kosovo for nine months with the Royal Canadian Mounted Police and the U.N.

At the time we were living in Orleans, Ontario. I was working for Crabtree & Evelyn and also busy with my business, Whitelight and the Trinity Table. Nine months is not a long time when you are busy with living and loving it.

I was in meditation one morning in my Angel/Fairy Room when I felt a presence hovering around me. I asked who it was and saw a vision of a name: "Tatiana." She was delightful and said she would be the communicator between John and me while he was away. Internet was not so great then, although I do have nine months of emails I hope to share with our grandchildren one day. Tatiana, this fairy, said that any information I wanted to share with John I could give to her while I was in prayer and she would transfer the information to him. Perfect. Just what I needed to feel close to him during our time apart. So each morning during meditation or prayer in my Angel Room I sent him thoughts, love and ADVICE.

I was doing this regularly until July of 2003, when I went to visit our daughter Amanda in Lugo, Spain, for a month. She was there for a year finishing up her doctorate degree. One evening I told her I needed to go to an internet cafe to email her dad. While there, I mentioned that Tatiana had given me a message I needed to give to him. Her face went white. "Mom, where did you get that name?" she asked.

I replied, "In prayer I have a guardian and she sends your dad and me messages; her name is Tatiana."

Amanda then proceeded to tell me that ever since she could remember she always said that if she had a daughter she would name her Tatiana. We both had goose bumps!

Years passed and one day Amanda announced that she was expecting. I sensed that was John's last mission. And so it is.

A week before Tatiana was born, a few friends and I were at Amanda's baby shower. Someone asked what she would name the baby. Her reply: "I am not sure, but if it is a girl,

Mark [her husband] likes the name Tatiana. But that is Mom's thing." I thought she had forgotten by then what she told me in Spain.

One of the attendees at the shower decided to look in the baby book for the meaning of names; "Tatiana" means Fairy Queen in Russian. Wonder of wonders.

Amanda then said, "We will know her name when we see her."

At last the day arrived and a baby girl was born. An hour into her first day on the planet, Amanda said a few names out loud but the baby did not open her eyes. Then, ever so softly, Amanda whispered, "Tatiana"... and the baby opened her eyes. Yes, she now has her name.

Tatiana is joy to all. One of the joys is the love we have for her as grandparents, and her love and acceptance for us. She calls me "Lil Lee" and John, her grandpa, she calls "Monka." That is all she calls him, and she adores him. We wondered why she calls him Monka. I Googled it, and in Kosovo, Monka is Monk.

John has eight archetypes exclusive to him: the Jester, the Knight, the Athlete, the Father, the Doubter, and, yes, you guessed it, the MONK. So if you do not believe in fairies, look back into your life; there is a story waiting to be told.

Just for today...

... let the Magic of Your Story have you.

DAY 50

The Spirit of Divine Grief

I have come to realize that when you lose a child you are birthing once again, as you enter into the death canal. I could not have done this sacred act if the collective had not midwifed.

Giving birth in this manner is a very sacred experience. Universal midwife skills are divine. There will never be anyone on this planet who does not experience grief.

It is only through this spirit that we unite and become one — the true essence of who we are, reflecting one another in our joy, our sadness. This is what keeps us human; a divine human.

Now it is time to live in sacred balance, to live life to the fullest, to feel everything.

Birth a new day, letting spirit have us.

Just for today...

... let the Spirit of Divine Universal Grief have you.

DAY 51

Do You Give?

Do you give, or always take?
Is the shadow of your beggar still awake?
Can you give freely your time, money, space?

If your answer is "No," you will meet yourself, face to face.
Is your life working you, or are you falling apart?
Do you never finish that which you start?
Are you repeating a pattern, and blaming the other?
Chances are it isn't your mother.

Give yourself freely, share when you can.
Love unconditionally, every child, woman and man.

Just for today…

… let the Spirit of Giving have you.

DAY 52

Oz

I need to go to the Land of Oz, click my heels,
my breath to pause.

I will see myself in all that is around me, my four survivors
they will surround me.

They will give me courage, a heart and brain, and when I return I will not be the same. Letting spirit have me... Now where are those red shoes?? Or maybe the silver they will deliver back to my innermost self... the fairy elf!

Just for today...

... let the Spirit of Playfulness have you.

DAY 53

Your Reality

Your reality comes from deep within you.
To create or change your world
Love endlessly,
Pray daily,
Give unconditionally,
Serve as if no one is watching.

Just for today...

... let the Spirit of Your Real Self have you.

DAY 54

For Give Ness

Forge ahead. Give to others. Rest in the assurance that we are not alone.

Forgiveness does not mean to forget.

Just for today...

... let Spirit have you in Forgiveness.

DAY 55

Awe of the Raw

No pills, no drills, no booze, no snooze, no shopping or hopping to avoid the pain.

Feeling the raw, but still in awe of all that surrounds us this day.

Letting Spirit have us…

…ALL of us.

DAY 56

Create

We create to be with Spirit, we are in Spirit to create.

At what cost is our creativity?

Do we shut out those we love?

Be creative today, but remember to include those around you while you are enjoying the moments of your creative self.

Be in harmony.

Just for today…

… let the Spirit of Creative Harmony have you.

DAY 57

Home

Home has a heart when the heart has a home.

My husband, John, and I are retired and home. It feels good to relax and feel.

It is beautiful to witness each other in our darkest moments and be able to say, "I am that."

Just for today, let Spirit have you in gratitude for family and friends.

Feel, feel, feel... for there is your freedom.

Just for today...

... let the Spirit of a Heartfelt Home have you.

DAY 58

Going to Sleep

Going to sleep now with loved ones on my mind...

Oh, the joy, for God is kind.
We will meet in paradise,
Speak only of love,
See the stars, the heavens above.
We will embrace,
Hold on to each other,
Bond finally as
Daughter and mother,
or father, brother.

Just for today...

... let the Spirit of Sleep have you.

DAY 59

God's Divine Plan

I sleep, I weep
For all life lost
And truly understand
God's divine plan.
In light and shadow
We are tossed
To face the glory
Of the beauty of all that was, is, will continue to be,
you, me, we...

Love never dies,
It just IS.

Just for today...

... let the Spirit of the Divine's Plan have you.

DAY 59+

A Bonus Day for Leap Year – A Day of Cookies!

Who does not love cookies? There are breakfast cookies, big chunk cookies, mini cookies – as kids we even knew the Cookie Monster.

So many of us now have digestive issues related to flour, corn, sugar, and other ingredients that are not healthy for us. It is difficult to find a scrumptious cookie recipe without those unhealthy ingredients. My good friend Lynn Mayer gave me this recipe from the Almond Board of California (www.almonds.com). She made a few substitutions to make them her own. Make them weekly for yourself, friends, and wee cookie monsters who visit.

Almond Chocolate Cookies (gluten-free, ultimate classic chocolate chip cookies) Makes 48 cookies.

625 ml (2 3/4 cups) almond flour (from whole almonds)
2 ml (1/2 tsp) salt
2 ml (1/2 tsp) baking soda

125 ml (1/2 cup) grapeseed oil

125 ml (1/2 cup) maple syrup

15 ml (1 tbsp) vanilla

125 ml (1/2 cup) dark chocolate chips (or 15 divided pieces of Lindt dark chocolate bars)

125 ml (1/2 cup) sliced almonds

125 ml (1/2 cup) coconut (optional)

Heat oven to 180° C (350° F). Line baking sheets with parchment paper. In a large bowl, combine almond flour, salt, and baking soda. In a medium bowl, combine grapeseed oil, maple syrup, and vanilla. Add to almond flour mixture and mix until thoroughly combined. Fold in chocolate chips and almonds. Spoon dough one heaping teaspoon at a time onto baking sheets and press down to flatten.

Bake for 7 to 10 minutes, until lightly golden. Let cookies cool on baking sheets for 20 minutes. (Lynn bakes them for 15 minutes at 325 degrees.)

Just for today…

… let the Spirit of a Yummy Cookie have you.

DAY 60

Ego

I have come to realize that blaming ourselves for what happens to others is a form of self-abuse. It is ego having its way with us.

If we truly believe that all is in divine order, that we have a sacred contract and that it is never our intent to harm anyone, then we can accept and stop blaming ourselves.

Our ego can relax, accept, and we can begin the healing process.

Just for today...

... let the Spirit of Letting Go of Ego have you.

DAY 61

Pandora's Box, the Gift of Hope

I remember when I was nine or ten years of age and I was chosen to play Pandora in a play. This play was called Pandora's Box. It is a memory that has stayed with me these many years. I have often contemplated the meaning of what was in that jar or box of Pandora's. It was not a coincidence when colleagues of mine, "Sisters of Light," gave me the title of Sister of Hope in 2001 as a gift from Archangel Uriel. This was given to me at a workshop with the Trinity Table in Fairfax, Virginia. They hold the lights of Sister Compassion, Sister Unity, Sister Love and Sister Peace.

In the last few years I have come to an understanding that Pandora's gifts are similar to my personal archetypes. If you saw my archetypal wheel, you would better understand this Sister of Hope — a queen who once wore the crown of a shameful mind. A thief who once had a deceitful nature. Ah, and my old friend the addict, who introduced me to my spiritual self. These now all live somewhere in the past, between forgetting and forgotten. Ah, there is hope for those of you still addicted, or feeling you do not have what it takes to make it in this world. Once you know yourself and are willing to change, miracles happen.

I give thanks to Caroline Myss for her work and teachings about how to live a symbolic life in reference to knowing thyself. Studying with Caroline, you soon learn everything is to be embraced through the lens of symbolism, and you begin to learn to stop taking others and yourself literally and seriously. I suggest you read *Sacred Contracts*, or another of her many books.

Pandora's name means "the giver of all." As you may already know, Pandora's box was really a jar — a jar filled with darkness, illness and plagues. What darkness resides in you? What makes you sick? What plagues you daily? Because of her curiosity, Pandora opened and unleashed these so-called gifts to the world. Only the gift of hope was not released from the jar.

Perhaps the jar can represent the container for our spirit, our mind and our body.

We need light and shadow to be whole — the light, the dark, the good, the bad, the ugly, the shadow, the feminine, the masculine. Balance. What is left in the jar that stifles this balance, that represses us from being whole? Everything passes — anger, delight, love, hate, sun, rain. The energy we have one day is electric, the next day dampened and drained.

What is in our container that can release us from total despair? Ah yes, Hope. We are familiar with "This too shall pass." That is the language of Hope. Hope is in the temple where your God meets you and sends you out into the world. On a global scale it is the balance of looking into someone eyes, no matter their religion, colour, race, beliefs or sex, and seeing them as your equal. Get out there — you can make a difference. The difference can be a Hope-filled attitude. It does not have to be enormous. Get out of your EGO (Edging God Out) and go where Spirit directs you.

What does Hope look like? Maybe it is the courage to forgive. Maybe it is the peace you bring to others. Maybe it is learning to trust again — yourself first.

I have been asked, "What do you think the world needs now?" My answer: "Hope." Hope lifts the darkness from your psyche; it allows you to open the jar within you.

You just never know what will inspire you when you open this lid. What will the Divine send you through this energy of Hope? Courage?

I strongly recommend you read Andrew Harvey's book, *The Hope: A Guide to Sacred Activism.* It will inspire you to live a symbolic life filled with positive change.

My gift to you this day is that you are filled with the wisdom of Hope, that your heart expands with Hope, and that you share this Hope with many. Like the loaves and fishes, allow Hope to multiply. Be in Hope as you commune within your community. As you break bread together, experience happy Hope.

Just for today...

... let the Spirit of Hope have you.

DAY 62

Love Poem from the Goddess

I am unravelling the old to stitch in the new.

I am weaving thyself around the fabric of my inner self.

I am threading the needle to blend shadow into thy light.

I am placing this wrapping of love onto my beloved's shelf.

When my beloved, this god/goddess who loves me
with defects,

Takes me down to breathe through me, shows me how my
willingness has a cause and effect,

I will dance in joy as I have come to realize all this unravelling,
weaving, threading has made me whole,

Casting this needle of light right through my soul.

Just for today…

… let Spirit have you.

DAY 63

I Believe

I BELIEVE.
I believe I can be thankful to the Earth and
be good to the Earth.
I believe I can be responsible.
I believe I can try to use less electricity.
I believe I can help save animals that are becoming extinct.

I believe I can help protect the animals,
the trees and all in our environment.
I believe I can ask for the help of others.
I believe that together we can try really hard to believe that
joining our talents we can ALL make a difference.

I believe, in you, in me...
WE BELIEVE that in joy we can live in HARMONY.

This was written with me by a group of four-year-olds at a workshop I gave many years ago. They believe in everything, and that all is possible.

Just for today...

... let the Spirit of Belief have you.

DAY 64

Emptiness

Emptiness is where I will rest on the waves of faith
Floating the crest of peace
Embracing the tides of compassion
With ripples of hope
As the jewels of sunlight sparkle through me.
I am empty, except
I am filled with the love from thee.
Empty from the ever–tormenting me.

Just for today…

…let Spirit have you.

DAY 65

Sharing

I am sharing myself today with nothing in return.
Can I allow the energy to flow
Without feeling I'm getting burned?
I have a desire to make a difference,
To follow the path of truth,
To "give in light and compassion,
Without taking and expecting redemption,"

— a quote from Ruth in The Bible

Letting go of our desire to give, with non-attachment, is a lesson few of us learn and understand. Our intent may be to give freely, but have we harvested that desire to let go... or are we still seeding, waiting for acceptance to grow?

Once we have an understanding of self-love and are able to give and receive (and I don't mean material stuff or ego longings), can we give without expecting something in return? Can we receive without wanting to sell a piece of ourselves?

Once we acknowledge that this giving is coming from something deep inside ourselves, from a sacred space, then it is free. Free from expectations. Spirit continues to live and breathe through us. Spirit has a voice. Living from our hearts (the eye of the needle) is one key, one step toward empowerment.

Just for today…

… let the Spirit of Sharing have you.

DAY 66

Fate/Destiny

When your stars are in alignment and your fate is plain to see,

Will you make conscious choices to follow your destiny?

If possible, go find a good astrologer. Find out your time of birth before you go. Allow the excitement of following the stars and planets in your chart to flow.
Use it as a road map.

Just for today...

...let Spirit have you when making choices;
be aware, be not afraid.

DAY 67

The Spirit of Women's Day

Happy Women's Day!

You are a woman on a mission.
You give yourself permission
To be all you want to be.
They do not know what you have been told,
To listen to the trinity three.
Because you do,
The energy runs through,
You are guided to listen to spirit, you do.
Yes, you are a woman on a mission —
Give yourself permission
To be ALL YOU CAN BE!
Happy Day, Goddess!

Just for today...

... let the Spirit of the Divine Feminine have you.

DAY 68

Grief

What is this weight that lies upon your heart today, child?
It is grief, so weep, weep, weep.
Did you think you would bypass this surgery?
You can only heal by entering your depths — the overflowing humanness of pain, love and acceptance.

As you weep, weep with gladness, sadness. Weep for the masses as no one bypasses this surgery. It will cut you but it will heal the whole of you. The holy of you.

Sleep now, child, for that, too, is time to peel back your ego and allow spirit to flow.

Just for today…

… let Spirit have you.

DAY 69

Change

Changing and seeing a new reality, if this one is not working for you, allows you to find new ways to see your life differently.

Do you want to be right or happy?

Your anger is Spirit's way of showing you to pay attention and make a shift.

Just for today...

... let Spirit have you.

DAY 70

The Now

Solitude of grace, let us face the now.
Let us heal our bodies, heal our hearts.
Let us not part from the vow to live in the now.

Just for today...

... let the Spirit of Healing have you.

DAY 71

The Spirit of Travel

You have the ability to travel to the four corners of the world today.

Hold on — it is a journey filled with hope and inspiration.

Close your eyes and imagine anything and everything.

Enjoy the joy of the journey.

Just for today…

… let Spirit have you and remember to Breathe.

DAY 72

Behind You

You cannot put anything behind you unless you walk through it.

Walk fearlessly.

Release any burdens from your past.

Letting go will create space for your new journey ahead.

Just for today…

… let the Spirit of Forging Ahead have you.

DAY 73

Grace

Clothe yourself with grace today.

Face yourself with love.

Stand in your power as you shout to the heavens.

Just for today...

... feel the Spirit of You below as well as above.

DAY 74

Bliss

Yes, it is possible to feel blessed beauty and bliss.

Nothing can stand in your way unless YOU allow it.
Feel the divine when you pray.
Feel the happiness when you plan your tomorrows.

Feel the awe of the raw when you feel your sorrows.
Feel the step with each new dance.
Feel the love with each new romance.

Feel the emotion when I tell you this:
You were born blessed, in beauty and bliss.

Just for today...

... enjoy Bliss.

DAY 75

Attitude

It doesn't matter what you do; it's the attitude you do it with.

Treat everything you touch today as a sacred object.

See everyone as the divine soul they are.

Work to serve and I promise you, all you do will be in gratitude.

Just for today...

... let the Attitude of Gratitude have you.

DAY 76

The Spirit of Saint Paddy's Day

The Irish are coming, the Irish are here.
What are you talking about my dear?
"Well, I's a Newfoundlander, don't you know?
Proud to be one, head to toe.
I'll kick up me heels, raise a little hell.
The fairy is coming out now, can't you tell?"
B'y, it must be spring you silly fool,
Now tell me a yarn, as you sit on your stool.
"Ah, yes b'y, life is grand,
Grateful I'm a NEWFIE and not from Japan."

Just for today…

…let living the Spirit of Your Roots have you.

DAY 77

The Spirit of Living

Stop looking to others to tell you how. When you take your last breath, it will be between you and the god/goddess of your understanding — the Universal Source. You will not have to ask, "Am I pretty enough? Did I do enough? Am I good enough?" Spirit will have you as you are.

Imagine, as you go about your routine, that today is between you and Spirit — no one else.

Live like no one is watching — only the God Source.

Just for today...

... let the Spirit of Living Out Loud have you.

DAY 78

The Eternal Om; Embracing Your Light and Your Shadow

Everywhere in Puri Taman Sari (in Bali), home of Mr. Prana and his family, there is an eternal Om.

I cannot help but wake up here; my spine binds to a dance, an electrical charge, romance with the heavens. As I sit in meditation this morning, my eyes take in sights I heavenly dreamed of: doves mating, butterflies as big as bats dancing (really!), rice fields humming, a bird song close by. A rooster telling us it is time to awaken, an orchestra surrounds my senses. Here I have no need to play the music on my iPod — music is alive everywhere! There is no need; just be. The floral (orchids, frangipani) abundance is within my gaze.

I understand now why those who travel with me on our yearly spiritual journeys awaken. Some become hostile even amongst this beauty — those whose inner work is just beginning. This energy moves in them, they become alert to self. This awakening is not for the faint of heart. Time here allows you to embrace the light of you, the shadow of you, everything becoming one. For some the shadow prefers to sleep; upon awakening, it transforms them.

This transformation changes you. How fast will you allow your life to change?

You do not have to travel as far as Bali to awaken to your eternal Om. Pay attention to the details today. There you will find your awakening.

Just for today…

… let the Spirit of Your Awakening have you.

DAY 79

The Spirit of the Spring Equinox

This is time for awakening and setting intentions for the rest of the year. Things have changed since New Year's Day, and your intentions might look quite different now that spring is in the air and the warmer seasons beckon.

Celebrate the balance of the night and day during this time of the year, and open the door to balance in other areas of your life, creating a positive rhythm for your dreams and aspirations. Tune in to the love that's in the air for all creatures to embrace.

This spring...

...let the Spirit of Your Intentions have you.

DAY 80

Open the Door; What Erupts in You?

What erupts in you? What makes you quake in your tracks?

I remember when I was young, before the age of twelve, I dreamt that I was in a country with volcanoes and ash and beauty everywhere. (I grew up in Newfoundland, which has its own beauty.)

I would have this dream while I was playing on Ocean Drive. I had thought at the time that the place was perhaps Hawaii. As I matured, I gave in to the illusion that it was a place from past life. Now I realize that it was not Hawaii but Bali.

Here I am today in Bali, amongst this splendor, the volcano and the ash. Everything is alive and growing abundantly.

I now understand that I am living that dream. We all can live our dreams — we only need to understand the fear that stops us. What erupts in you that slows you down? What fears entangle you?

What you fear at this moment is a memory from yesterday; it is something for which you have a frame of reference. Today this fear does not exist — only your memory of it. The only thing you need to fear is your past, so be open to all possibilities TODAY! Open the door and allow the flow to erupt in you.

Just for today...

... open your inner Door.

DAY 81

The Garden

I sit in a garden; it flowers with hope.

The trees are filled with abundance,

The soil is rich in healing,

The sun is sending waves of love.

The air is filled with awakenings. This sacred space, this garden of tranquility.

Just for today...

...let the Spirit of Your Own Garden have you.

DAY 82

Surrender

Surrender any former notion of a single Divine Presence today; We, You, Me, Thee are an expanded awareness.

We are a collective consciousness with the oneness of creation; we are one unified body of Love.

Just for today…

… let Spirit have you.

DAY 83

The Judge

We judge people not by the words they use but by the actions they take.

Find something good today about a person you are judging. You will then feel less separated from them.

If we spent just 5 percent of our time seeing the good in others and not the bad, we would become more unified with the rest of humanity.

Just for today…

…let the Spirit of Non-Judgment have you.

DAY 84

Nothing/Everything

You come into this world with nothing, you leave with nothing, but you are everything and everyone.

You come into this world from love, and you return to love.

Just for today…

…let the Spirit of Love have you.

DAY 85

Invoking the Seven Directions

As we awake each morning, breathing in a new day, and put our feet on the floor, we are filled with the divine knowledge that we have one more chance for a brand new day, a brand new NOW.

We have an opportunity to live our highest potential today.

Blessings surround us, and by choice we can see, feel, smell, touch the joy around us.

I cannot stress enough the importance of a daily ritual. This ritual does not have to be sitting in a corner with a candle burning and Om-ing for an hour. Just an altar in our environment alters our consciousness. Burning incense calls in the essence of Spirit.

In the morning, being in the present moment with my feet firmly on the floor, I take delight in burning incense to alert my consciousness and bring in the seven directions so that I may feel the connection to the God Source. I am aware that this God Source never leaves me. There are times, however, I leave God.

Invoking the Seven Directions

Facing east with arms held high we invoke the angelic being Uriel, The Light of God, who shows the clarity, the light in any person, place or situation. Uriel shines light on all.

Facing south with arms held high we sing the praises of the angelic being Gabriel, who shows the strength of all those with whom we surround ourselves this day, saying, "Gabriel, The Messenger, because we choose to be alert in this moment, thank you for sending us messages through a person, a place or a situation, because we have chosen to be witnesses to our lives." We choose to live in non-judgment and know that the strength of Gabriel cloaks us with the knowledge that we have compassion for ourselves and all those who enter our thoughts.

Moving and facing west with arms held high we are attuned to the angelic being Raphael, The Healer of mind, body and spirit. As we feel his healing energy seeping through our cells, our memories, and the spirit of who we are, we recognize that we are in the moment of wellness. Gratitude flows through the crown into the body and into the core of the universe. Into this core we feel our bodies take in the iron of the planet, which is so important to our health.

With reverence we move to the north, and with arms held high we are filled with the joy of the presence of the angelic being Michael; he who is most like God. In this present moment we are filled with the strength and the wisdom beyond the ages. This strength empowers us to live a courageous life.

With arms held to the heavens we say, "AS ABOVE," arms to the ground, "SO BELOW," arms wrapped around self, "I AM THAT I AM."

Just for today...

...let the Spirit of the Seven Directions have you.

DAY 86

To Be Right or Happy

Today began in grace, then tears on my face.

Nothing shattering, just a splattering of a worn ego thrown in my face.

Do I want to be right, or do I want to be happy?

Come on answer, be snappy!

I want to be right but it's not worth the fight, so I will shed the tears, without any fears, and then when they are released I will feast in the knowing that Spirit had me.

Yes, I can be happy and let go of what I thought I did know.

Just for today…

…let Spirit have you.

DAY 87

We Are All God's Creators

We are in creation because we are creating.
We cannot be otherwise.

We are in communion within our community when we are breaking bread together, symbolically sharing, communicating and DOING.

Creativity flows through you — see it, speak it, feel it, own it, DO it... Share it!

You will note that your seven chakras are symbolized here. Your chakras are the organs of your soul.

Flow, see, speak, feel, own, do, share.

Just for today...

...be a God Creator.

DAY 88

The Spirit of Freedom

As we enter into this sacred season of Easter, let us remember the man, Jesus, who

walked his talk; who surrendered, rejoiced and transformed himself.

He showed us how we also can rise from our ashes and be free.

Just for today…

… let the Spirit of Freedom have you.

DAY 89

The Spell Has Been Broken

The spell has been broken. Here is my token.
If you continue to live in your ancestral dream
Your world will be dark, bitter, unclean.
Wake up, wake up, for you have missed the mark.
Love, forgiveness, compassion are the wands to open your heart.

Sometimes we have to walk away from old family traditions — beliefs that do not serve our highest good.

Just for today…

… let the Spirit of Broken Spells have you.

DAY 90

The Spirit of Stepping Up

Step up, take charge of your life; and I don't mean the two-step.

Are you dancing with destiny and allowing yourself to be fated by your thoughts and the actions and spells of others? Are you sitting in a deep sadness? Are you filled with regret and illusion?

Step up — you have a predetermined date with destiny. Your future is calling. Dance to the rhythm of your own drum. Beat down those ill-fated illusions you have surrounded yourself with. Life is not a fantasy. You are a co-creator; now go create the life you want.

Just for today…

… Step Up to Your Life.

DAY 91

The Spirit of Self-Esteem

Be kind, gentle and compassionate, but most of all, don't take anyone else's junk from their trunk. Allow them to dump it, but not on you. You are much too special for that garbage.

Just for today…

… let the Spirit of Self-Esteem have you.

DAY 92

This Moon

This moon, behold, you have me in your grasp.

The sight of you, my breath so quickly passes from my lungs
to the air to reach you there in all your glory and shine.
You speak your message, of loving ourselves, the Divine.

You hold my emotions in balance,
I am in laughter this moment, or shall I weep in joy, for now,
nothing is broken?
I am filled up, let us drink from this cup,
Your energy, your reflection, as it spills itself into the flow
Of the everlasting glow of time.
For now you are mine as I witness your beauty.
Monthly you are always here.

Pay attention to the monthly full moon. What message does she have for you?

Write your messages down, and in a year you will have twelve valuable lessons.

If it is the New Moon, start a list of to-dos for this month only. At the end of the year you will see how much you have accomplished.

Just for today…

…let the Spirit of the Message from Mother Moon have you.

DAY 93

I Pray

I am fully awake to all there is this day.
Let the nature of Spirit have me, I pray.
I will light three candles on my altar
One for the world, one for myself,
and anything else Spirit directs me to alter.
For in this consciousness I am aware and alert
That through prayer with Divine, I help chaos avert.

Just for today...

... let the Spirit of Your Own Prayers have you.

DAY 94

Feeling Alone, or a Lonely Feeling?

Someone once mentioned to me that she was feeling alone and I asked her if it was a lonely feeling. Is it a longing? I personally do not have a reference point for feeling lonely or feeling alone, and I was intrigued. When John was away on his missions with the U.N. it never occurred to me that I was alone or lonely. I guess it helped that I knew he was somewhere in the world and we had a commitment and a loving bond. We had a daughter and her family in New Brunswick, another in Ottawa, my parents and siblings in Alberta.

It had me thinking about all those who do feel alone — the longing for togetherness. What is it they are really wanting? I have always felt that there was an energy around me, a number of them actually, and have sensed them since I was a child and never questioned their love. Because of this love force, this abundance, there was a deep understanding that I am never alone. I am one with all.

Imagine feeling separated from that. Yes, there have been times of despair, panic or uncertainty, but I always knew "this too shall pass."

To those of you out there feeling alone, lonely, I hold you in my heart, my thoughts, my prayers. I and many others are with you. You are not alone. You are loved because you exist. You are loved because you are loving. You are loved because you ARE YOU.

Just for today...

...let Spirit have you.

DAY 95

Mom

Written for my mother on her seventy-fifth birthday:

You're the key that opens our hearts
When we feel we are falling apart,
The sunshine that melts our fears,
The curtain that hides our tears.

You're the rhythm in our steps,
The creator when we are doing our best.
You're the trickster in our very laughs,
The artist when we are re-creating our pasts.

Your hedonist abounds when you are clowning around,
And the shopping sprees,
when you are with us, that have such glee.
You're the queen in your sacred space,
You have taught us: appreciate love, live NOW, why wait?

You're the fairy who speaks with joy.
You love us equally; your girls, your boys.
Derek, who was willing to pass,
One day will welcome you with open arms, at last, at last.

You're the wife to a man who adores you.
There has been no one else since or before you.
You're an employee to Stella, but more of a mother,
For her wisdom tells her there is no other.

You helped your boy Al climb mountains, the highest peak!
Never a word of doubt did you speak.
You're a true friend to all you embrace,
For you live with non-judgment, with dignity and grace
You give them your truth, face to face.

Ah, Mom, you are the sweetness of the rose,
The compassion of Mary
The beloved queen; Queen of the Fairies.

They say,
It is not what she has nor what she does that expresses
the worth of a woman, it is who she IS,
Divine Grace.

If you have a mother, write something to her today. Look at her through the lens of archetypes. Who is she? How did she live her best life? Even if she is now in the spirit world, write to her anyway; she is still witnessing you in her new home.

Just for today...

... give to your mother.

DAY 96

To Judge

To judge another without compassion,
to judge with your anger,
to judge without knowing all the details of that
person's circumstances,
is a reflection of your own insecurities, your ego, your life.

Judging to such an extent as to speak in anger of someone
is possibly why our bodies are sick, our love-lives are not
flourishing, our finances are in scarcity. Just for today,
hold up a mirror.

Just for today...

... let Spirit have you.

DAY 97

Are You the One?

Are you the one to make a difference
When others are weeping;
Their homes, their lives leaking?
Do you think you are different?

Are you the one to live a congruent life
When there are those around you who feel they must give up their fight?

Are you the one to hold the space?
When chaos reigns, can you be in grace?

Are you the one?
When spirit calls, will you accept the challenge or will you run?
And if you run, will it be to thyself, where it all had begun?

Just for today…

…let the Spirit of Making a Difference have you.

DAY 98

I Will My Will

I will my will...
To stop looking, so I can see
To stop talking, so I can hear
To stop receiving, so I can give
To eat healthy, so I can continue to live.

Just for today...
I will stop running, so I can stand still
And open my heart to Spirit's will.

Just for today...

... will your will to let Spirit have you.

DAY 99

What Now, NOW What?

Why do we feel that we have to DO something of greatness? Can we not just BE with spirit?

How about we only came to this lifetime to sit and enjoy a good cup of tea, smell the tea leaves, taste the essence of the tea, and thank all those who brought it to our door — the farmer, the worker, the trucker, etc.? How about in one moment in time we are filled with such gratitude for that tea that we feel the essence of all those who are with us in spirit as we drink that tea? We send them love and joy. In that moment we realize there is no separation. I. Am. That.

Maybe this is our mission and all we are here for, to have a moment in time to send out that love. Or we just might be running a tea company. Whatever it is, we are living our highest potential — BEING, not DOING.

Just for today…

… let the Spirit of BEING have you.

DAY 100

Sisterhood

A bond was formed from our parents' seed
I see you, I see me.

The blood that runs through our veins the same.
The love we share, forever remains.

Just for today…

… if you have a sister, tell her you love her.

DAY 101

The Joy of Menopause

I will not change the lines on my face
For this would remove my past
There would be no trace
I do not feel I am losing my memory
There are things I have let go of
In this moment, my intuition is plenty
I will allow myself to feel I am drained
Let the energy flow, then less the pain
They say I have become rather bitchy
You would to, if you were always itchy
I am the woman I dreamt I would be
Free at last, to be ME
In my sacred place, I move from my thoughts to my heart

With grace,
This is where I heal — Thank you, Body
For now, I feel.

Just for today…
… let the Spirit of Aging have you.

DAY 102

Faith of Your Business

This message is not only for those of you in a business but for those of you in the business of living. How much faith do you have in the economy these days? Are you blaming the economy? Are you feeling humiliated because you have done all this work and feel you deserve more?

We are presently losing the world we grew up in. That is a fact — look around you. This is our fate. Our destinies are the choices we now make about how to handle all that is going on. Fate is essentially unavoidable; destiny is what you make of what fate gives you. Destinies are created when we build businesses with self-esteem based on our creative selves, not based on what our culture tells us to do. When we are able to act on these choices without the fear of humiliation, then we have the ingredients for the destinies of our businesses, which include the capacity to confront our expectations. It is for us to make choices as to what empowers us versus what disempowers us. Fate is run by the power of a frightened ego.

What are our expectations in regards to our businesses? We need to be clear about what our expectations are and whether we have faith in them.

Destiny is not for the faint of heart. It takes soul stamina to run a business these days. Our inner guidance says, "Give up" or "Try something new." The Fate of any business is mass-produced; Destiny is in our individual choices. Where are our treasures? There we will find our hearts. Are our hearts in our businesses? Fate observes what we are doing. Destiny lives and creates new ideas within our businesses. Fate says, "Give up!" while Destiny says, "I release the desire to know the outcome, but will continue with the faith I have in myself to serve and be served." (I developed my understanding of Fate versus Destiny through a course taught through the Caroline Myss Education Institute.)

I grew up with both parents working in retail, and I worked in marketing for fifteen years, was a sales representative for twelve years, and finally now work as a coach/networker/connector. I have learnt twelve valuable lessons that I wrote about many years ago when I was in Bali, which are the next two entries, days 103 and 104. These lessons inspired me and taught me that we do have what it takes to live our highest potential; we only have to believe in ourselves.

Just for today...

... let Faith in Your Destiny have you.

DAY 103

1 to 6 of the "12 Steps," Lilly-Style

1. Do not take yourself so seriously.

2. You are worthy. As above, so below.

3. Speak only truth. Your truth.

4. Always be at home, no matter where you are. The home has a heart, when the heart has a home.

5. Be more childlike — this is where you create and manifest.

6. Daily rituals are not work when you live in the moment.

You, me, we — trinity three

Just for today…

… let the Spirit of Your Personal 12 Steps have you.

DAY 104

7 to 12 of the "12 Steps," Lilly-Style

7. Relationships are but a reflection of you, ever holding a mirror to your greatness.

8. Respect the energy resources of others; allow them and yourself to go underground when needed. That is where you will choose to rise again.

9. Travel inside of your heart often; you will unite with souls and embrace what you cannot see.

10. Your highest potential is to be in unity with the divine self.

11. Your hopes, dreams and wishes can manifest. BELIEVE!

12. We are all connected. The air you breathe today, someone in Bali breathes tomorrow.

Just for today...

... get on with the business of living a Congruent Life.

DAY 105

Discussions, Under the Wisdom Tree

I remember my teacher, Caroline Myss, asking, "Why do you think you deserve anything?" I did not understand her message at the time, but I am finally receiving it.

We assume that if we are good — if we do this or say that — we deserve to be treated in a certain way. Why? What about living to serve? And I do not mean from the Servant archetype, through which we can act as slaves.

How about the thought that we are holding the abundance for ourselves and others? We are holding gifts for others. These gifts are plentiful, and if we are not balanced enough to accept them from Spirit, others hold them for us. So instead of saying to ourselves, "I deserve this," how about instead saying, "I accept this from the one who has been holding it for me because I was unable to contain it"? Then the giving becomes a serving to others, dishing out what was theirs to begin with. Spirit fills us up with all we could need, but sometimes we are unable to accept it due to timing.

I have been told that I give too much, but I have always felt I have enough. Because I am full, I give freely. I ask myself each time I give, "What is my intent behind the giving?" If I am selling myself, and that has happened, then I am not freely giving. Once I understood that I give what I have been holding for others until they decided they were ready, then it became a message of service. So today, instead of "I deserve," how about "I serve"?

Just for today...

... let the Spirit of Service have you.

DAY 106

Morning Rituals

In the middle of a ritual I realized that was what it was: a morning ritual. Since moving into my sixties I seem to have started something. I had been oblivious to this ritual until I caught myself singing a poem:

"I have cream for my dry body, cream for my cracked lips, cream for my dry hair and my sagging tits... Cream for my aging hands, and creams for my face, God Almighty I am going to cream myself from the human race into outer space!"

I just wanted to share this laugh. Yes, I realize people are still suffering, but some days we need a good tummy laugh to begin our day.

Have a day filled with laugher, rituals and joy.

Just for today...

... let the Spirit of Rituals have you.

DAY 107

A Day of "What If?"

What if for today you did not take yourself so seriously?
What if you did not take what others say so personally?
What if you did your work with joy instead of complaints?
What if, in the rain, you saw the beauty, the moisture, the gain?
What if the pain in your heart were really an awakening – a brand new start?
What if you greeted everyone you see today with hello and saw their halo?
What if you used your words with the intent to heal instead of defending what you think is real?
What if instead of rushing you stopped to breathe and sent a whisper to the breeze?
What if?

Just for today…

… let the question of "What if?" have you.

DAY 108

Following the Light

It's a sunny day, and this guy behind me is swearing at me because I will not move into traffic (because I cannot see; the sun is in my eyes). I finally see I am clear, and turn left onto Ottawa Street heading home, while noticing the guy is still giving me the hand signs. I think, "Oh fudge!" and behold, the bottom of my car hits the street. Yep, the whole underneath falls. I start laughing, and cannot stop laughing as I know my car is upset also.

You should have seen that guy in the vehicle behind me. I thought his face was gonna blow. Anyway, I left the car in the church driveway (good spot — it didn't have a prayer), and I walked home. The car went to the garage.

Hope and prayers helped. As for me, I am still laughing. Life is funny. So are cars and hand signals.

You are following the light home and there will always be someone cursing it — such is the journey of consciousness!

Just for today...

... let the Spirit of Humour have you.

DAY 109

Tutu

A few years ago, on one of my many trips to Bali, I was blessed to be in Ubud at the "Quest for Global Healing" conference. Bishop Desmond Tutu was the guest speaker, and as I sat and listened to this divine teacher, I was inspired to write these words:

As Tutu Speaks

As Tutu speaks, the bird sings,
The wisdom of the universe,
Spirit does bring.

We are wonderfully and fearlessly made,
None of us an afterthought.
We are all miracles, now ready to save.

God knew the divine he set forth.
You can feel it rise within you.
You are beautiful, filled with your own worth.

Have you ever watched an orchestra when the ring does happen?
A simple ring, ding, ding,

As with this simple ring, we are all here for a reason,
To enjoy all the seasons.

God weeps when you hide from your marvelous self.
He will not rest until you see yourself through his eyes.
Then and only then can he guide you with pride.

Remember the Buddha within — "the God in me respects the God in you."
And it is here that You and Me become We.
Take seriously that we are all God Carriers.
We are loveable because God loves us.
Grace is free.

As Tutu speaks,
God says, "I am no one except you."
I realize that what I have longed for is here;
I no longer seek.

The angels ask us this day, "Are you in rhythm with life in and around you?
Are you in the now? Are you able to create joyfully?
Are you a God Carrier, creating God?"

Now, Go Create God.

Just for today...

... let the Spirit of Co-Creating have you.

DAY 110

Puri Taman Sari

I return to Puri Taman Sari in time to witness my spiritual son's baby's ground-touching ceremony. This ceremony takes place when the newborn is three months old.

Agung Wah and Agung Agus are Agung Prana's sons. I am blessed to live with a Balinese family and learn their ways of living and giving.

The three months ground-touching ceremony involves the umbilical cord collected at birth, dried and wrapped in white cloth. This breaks the final bond to the four brothers who accompany the baby through birth and the first few days of life. The four brothers sound much like the four survival archetypes we struggle with in our culture — Child, Victim, Saboteur and Prostitute. Perhaps if we were to follow this magical healing, we, too, would live in harmony with these four constants — our power source, they live in our first three chakras.

To learn more about these, be sure to pick up or Google "Caroline Myss, Sacred Contracts." It will change your life. She offers online courses on this subject.

Just for today…

…let the Spirit of Learning have you.

DAY 111

Shankari

Upon awakening at Shankari's Retreat,
my senses are mesmerized.

Sounds of frogs, a rooster and other birds singing
their mantras to the heavens.

A gecko (a small lizard) perched above my head somewhere
sings in the morning with seven sounds of "gecko, gecko..."
If Agung Prana were here, he would advise me
this is a good omen.

Smells of champak incense mix with the richness of damp earth from last night's rain. I am surrounded by details of romance that only Shankari the Alchemist could manifest.

Bali lace surrounds the bed that housed my body for the journey of divine sleep, frangipani soap to wash away yesterday's energy, lavender shampoo to sooth the cells of hair that has been frolicking in the Bali Sea.

And the sights! Butterflies the sizes and colours of which can bring out the artist in many of us, even those of us who have never held a palette. Then the shocking pink bougainvillea, the banana trees, and in between this tropical growth, delightful hanging birds of paradise everywhere as far as my eye can see. All this and my day is just getting started.

I wonder what nutritious delights Bagus (whose name means "good") will have prepared in the kitchen with Chef to energize my body. Chai tea or Bali coffee? Pinang goreng (fried banana fritters), bubur sum-sum (creamy rice pudding with palm sugar) or maybe nasi goreng (fried rice).

Experience this with me, in eternal bliss with me, anytime.

Just for today... ...

... let the Spirit of Your Senses have you.

DAY 112

The Spirit of Earth Day

Happy Earth Day!

Realize that every day is a celebration and an opportunity to give thanks.

Go clean up any garbage on your sidewalk.

Stay away from water bottled in plastic.

Go outside, no matter what the weather.

Enjoy the fresh air, the rainy days.

Plant a new tree.

Donate to the Earth Day network.

Make every day Earth Day.

Just for today…

… let the Spirit of Thanksgiving and Gratitude have you – Happy Earth Day!

DAY 113

A Question

I asked John a question,
I'll never forget,
"What would you change about me,
From when we first met?"
An ease came over him,
Silent and pure,
"Humility I'd give you,
for this I am sure."
HUMILITY, a word,
The meaning was dense,
So the Bible I searched
To see what it meant.

There it was,
So big and so bold,
"Pay attention," said Sarah (10:13),
Of this I was told.
Learning the lessons,
That was a must.
To humble myself, a new word, trust...

To live at my best,
The answer was there, my eyes did adjust,
Now here was something, a challenge, a test.

Wisdom, it is said, comes at a price.
You don't just wake up and turn on the light.
Once you're committed to learn and to grow,
The universe has answers, "You reap what you sow."

Just for today...

... let the Spirit of Humility have you.

DAY 114

Embrace Your Magic

Embrace your magic,
It's yours for real,
deny not yourself nor the light that you feel.

Embrace your essence, the glow that you are.
Question not, for it comes from Estar.

Embrace your divinity, the trinity three,
live from your soul and you become we.

Embrace your palace, the energy of light
Wisdom is yours now, spread out, take flight.

Embrace your magic,
Feel the suspense,
Your life is changing, your shadow is spent.

Just for today...

... let the Spirit of Your Inner Magic have you.

DAY 115

SO, Soulfully Letting Go

Until you change your story, your troubles will follow. And they will not pass as quickly as you would like.

I feel compassion for you, but really, until you change your story and are willing to Let Go, your troubles will not change.

SO, you have a bad day. SO, you have a blissful day. SO. This too shall pass.

Everything in and around us is in constant change — our cells, our brain tissue, our nervous system. We awake, we sleep, the sun rises, the sun sets... on and on. Change...

SO, why do we hold on, knowing this will pass? Allow the flow of change and respond with SO, Soulfully. Let go; let God.

SO, are you in one of the four survival archetypes: "Whyyyy?" (Child), "Ya, but..." (Victim), "What if?" (Saboteur), "Well maybe..." (Prostitute)?

Create, let go, have fun, pay attention to the energy of your astrology chart, let go, bad Mars day, let go, blissful Venus day,

enjoy, let go, SO, this too shall pass. Monitor yourself as the tides... in, out, enjoy the moment, flow, let go, SO, today have as many soul-filled experiences as you can,
then let go. SO.

Just for today...

... let the Spirit of SO, Let Go, have you.

DAY 116

You're Invited

WHAT: Love-In

WHERE: In your heart chakra

WHEN: Now

DRESS CODE: Your beauty

DIRECTIONS: Go inward, take a breath

Just for today…

… let the Spirit of Inner Love have you.

DAY 117

Your Victim, Your Joy

I thought I had lived through everything. But there are still days when I am unbalanced — that knee-jerk reaction, all because someone said something I did not like. Gee, I was sure I had dumped those feelings in the dumpster years ago. Alas, that person is in my life to bless me with grace — grace to witness myself once again from the Victim — not the light, but the shadow. It was a simple conversation, talking about Power Up Your Life, the planning, etc., then came the dynamite that set my butt on fire: "Nobody can take you seriously, Lilly; not when you are in your Fairy. You could never talk to the corporate world. You are not real, you are not serious, you have not suffered enough. You get on people's nerves with your Joy."

All these years holding that space, and in one moment, down I went. Anger first, then awe at my reaction, then the tears. "What is the matter with me? Boohoo, nobody likes me."

Really friends, what is with this environment we have created in which we cannot relate to someone unless they are in their

Victim? You want my Victim? You want me to tell you about my suffering before you accept that I have lived my shadow and my light? Okay.

I am in a 12-step program. And by the way, you know all the books you are reading? At least half of them are based on this wondrous program. You want me to tell you about raising a child who is bipolar? Maybe you want me to share with you the pain of losing a brother to suicide? Or the pain of watching your husband on chemotherapy for two years, every three weeks, while your children are two years and six months old? Or how about living in a trailer on your own with one daughter, while the other daughter is in the hospital with ANOTHER suicide attempt? John and I were separated for a short time while I got my life together. How about being so frightened as a child that up until seventeen years of age, whenever a certain person looked at me sternly I immediately urinated. Talk about fear of authority.

Okay, okay. Enough already! Yes, suffering is real! Living your life, loving it regardless of what you experience, finding the Joy in ALL things and then living that Joy are also REAL. The wings on my back have much better consequences for me as a human being than the heart of an angry heroine. Yes, I have courage, Yes, I have learned to LAUGH at myself. You ARE Joy! You are not getting off this planet alive, so you might as well enjoy the ride. Yes, yes, feel the pain that life brings you, but look at the wonders of the wounds that make you YOU. For example, if I had not had the experience of addiction, I would not be equipped to help others face the destructiveness of their Addict. The message today is to relate to yourself in Joy. Your child within, even in difficult times, can choose to be in the light.

Live your life with Purpose on Purpose. Let us learn to relate with Joy.

Just for today…

… let the Spirit of Your Victim be in the Light.

DAY 118

Joy

I asked my love, what gives you Joy?
My legs, so I may walk this day.
You have no legs;
Now what gives you Joy?
To watch a robin
As it feasts on its prey.
But you have no eyes to see this day;
Now what gives you Joy?
To hear the song of a voice so clear,
Its melody touches my heart as it reaches my ear.
But you have no ears to hear this day;
What gives you Joy?
To smell the lavender as it dances in the wind,
The scent of the roses, as their blossoms begin.
But you have no smell to breathe this in;
So what gives you Joy?
I ask you again.
It is the taste of strawberries on a summer's eve,
Their flavour and texture enhanced

With a hint of spearmint leaves.
Ah, but I say unto you, lover of hope,
On this day your taste buds have faded from
when we last spoke;
So I ask you again, what gives you Joy?
Ah, teacher, I understand, as I sit here, barely a man,
I am more than the sum of all of my parts,
The Joy is inside me, I feel it, my heart.
In the stillness, my essence, I embrace God's delights,
For here is the Joy, it is ME, I am Light.

Just for today…

…let the Spirit of Your Joy have you.

DAY 119

There Is a Hero in Every War

There is a hero in every war,
A war in every hero.

There is a tree in every seed,
A seed in every tree.

There is laughter in every tear,
A tear in every laugh.

There is a dream in every soul,
A soul in every dream.

There is a death with every birth,
A birth with every death.

There is pain with every life,
Life with every pain.

There is joy in every day,
A day well lived is joy.

There is silence in this moment,
A moment in this silence.

There is God in everything,
Everything in God.

Just for today…

…let the Spirit of All Your Moments have you.

DAY 120

The Quiet Knight

"I leave today for Kosovo." The year is 2001.
"I am aware of dangers, but my soul, its mission has just begun.
This United Nations-governed entity within its sovereign land
I will help protect, from the city of Pristina,
as only a police officer can."

"I have been home for a while," the Knight does speak,
"Another mission, I long to seek.
East Timor is calling, for its independence it is longing,
Known as its 'institutional foundations for independence.'
I leave now, to help reconstruct the infrastructure,
To bring peace,
As a peace officer to those who bleed upon their fence."

The Quiet Knight returns,
But a hole in the planet within him still burns.
He has heard of Haiti, this Francophonic independent
nation in the Americas.

This island of corruption, of dictators who affect the national
life of everyone.
He leaves once again, to help with the fight.
A mission, a peacekeeping operation,
Will he succeed? It is better to try than be in fear; the fear
would be the omission.

Retired now from the RCMP, nine months of seeding tranquilly,
A birth of ideas it comes to pass,
"Afghanistan is calling, another mission, this one my last.
This country, this crossroads between the East and the West
Hope for a better day for Afghanistan, to help its people,
Will I stand up for the task?
I will not know, until the last of the sorrow, perhaps tomorrow?"

Just for today...

... be your own Hero, let Spirit have you.

DAY 121

The Spirit of Marriage

It has occurred to me how my spirituality is much like my forty-year relationship and marriage to John.

In 1973 I felt a pull to this man and thus began a daily dance with rituals of romance.

Similarly, in 1991, I felt and came to believe in a power greater than myself and began daily rituals of prayer and worship. Don't get me wrong — I had always believed in God, but I did not have a daily ceremony to invite the energy in, except for the weekly trek to church on Sundays.

I began with a daily serenity prayer upon waking, then prayers throughout the day. A meeting of like-minded people was a weekly event, and the connection to Spirit was a comradeship that was seductive. Much like the daily phone calls to my new lover and our weekly dates to a movie or out dancing — something we had in common.

Like any relationship we enter into, it was all-consuming and life seemed brighter, bigger and dazzling. I remember that no matter what chaos was around me, all seemed easier, smoother and lighter; anything was possible. Then came the moment of making a vow — a commitment to honour, love and obey; to live with no judgment, to feel compassion and to allow each other to live together while still each being masters of our own souls.

With my spiritual practice, daily rituals became a habit: up every morning, light a candle, read a prayer or thought-for-the-day. I was planting seeds, just as John and I were planting seeds in our marriage and we began to have our children. In my spirituality, I began to give birth to reiki; I came to understand energy. In our marriage, I began to understand the life and responsibility of a child. Here is where we begin to feed and nurture. There were days when I would want to run away from home due to the work, and yes, there were days when I did not want to hear about God or energy or even look at another book.

As our family grew, so did my soul, and it began to hear the call deep into self. And as the girls prepared to leave home I began to leave old ideas behind and begin my journey out into the world seeking wisdom.

In our marriage, I learnt lessons that were, and continue to be, valuable assets to the couple we are and to the coupling of my soul. The blending of harmony, peace and joy.

We are committed to stay on course no matter what the day brings. There will always be shifts, differences of opinion, boredom and even anger. Isn't that the journey we are on? To embrace the Divine in each other, to allow the lover to grow with a free spirit and a free will?

Spirit knows I go nowhere without the breath of life; my marriage is aware I go nowhere without the breath of love.

Just for today...

... let the Marriage of Your Soul have you.

DAY 122

The Spirit of Integration

I am, I am, you are me,
Let US Be, LET US BE.
I am playing, I am staying
Into the music of this delight.
I am Heaven; I am shaken into the realm of height.
Hold on with all your might.
I am joy, I am joy,
I am Girl, I am Boy, and I am Child,
I am Sage,

I have no name, I have no age.

I am holy, I am whole,
I am empty, so I'm told.
I am filling, because I'm willing
TO BE, TO BE, TO BE.
I am rising, I am diving
Into the mist of this bliss.
The stars above, the stars within,
The stars of the heart, the stars apart.

You are here, we are there,
Oh GOD, you are Me, We are Thee.
It is all a joke, we can laugh aloud.
We are shining, we are drowning
Into a dream, into a theme,
Into a story, into the holy,
Into the depth of oneness.
I was a movie, was no one.
I was everyone, I was here,
I was there,

It is happening, it is evolving, and it is revolving,
The moment is NOW, take a breath and
BREATHE, BREATHE, BREATHE.

You have arrived HOME!

Just for today...

...let the Spirit of Coming Home to Self have you.

DAY 123

The Spirit of Heavy

When you are feeling heavy in your pain,
From your ego reframe.
When you are feeling trapped,
Reach out with your arms; your comfort from
others you wrap.
Lift the weight of your ego self.
Find ways to increase love, dust yourself from the shelf.
When you are feeling heavy, go play, find an elf.
The elementals will always be around to show you how to love
yourself.

Just for today...

... Go Play.

DAY 124

The Spirit of Inner Beauty

Our inner beauty shines through in simple ways.

a smile to someone hurting
a helping hand to someone in need
a caress on a child's cheek
a phone call when someone is in pain

Just for today...

... let the Spirit of Your Inner Beauty shine.

DAY 125

The Spirit of Being Content

"My crown is in my heart, not on my head;
Not decked with diamonds and Indian stones,
Nor to be seen.
My crown is called, Content."
— William Shakespeare.

Contentment is a gift from nature.
We can feel it when we least expect it.
Once we learn who we are, what our needs are,
How to ask for help, how to say no, how to say yes,
It is liberating to be satisfied/content.

Just for today…

… let the Spirit of Contentment have you.

DAY 126

The Spirit of Being Happy

I am HAPPY.

I did not just HAPPEN to BE. I was created with love and glee.

Just for today…

… let Spirit have you.

DAY 127

The Spirit of a Hero/Heroine

Go ahead, be your own hero/heroine;
Take a risk today.
Put your desires/dreams into action;
Willingness is all that is needed.
Go on, let your light shine.

Just for today…

… let the Spirit of Your Inner Hero have you.

DAY 128

The Spirit of Motherhood

Happy Mother's Day!

To all those who have not given birth, who are estranged from their children, who have lost their children to the spirit world, may the pain crack you open and may the Divine Mother in you give birth to all of your creativity and inspiration. Happy Mother's Day.

Just for today…

… let the Spirit of the Divine Mother have you.

DAY 129

The Spirit of Sorrow

Oh God, I do not want to feel this pain today;
I will keep it at a distance for just one more day.
This sorrow, yes, tomorrow.
Perhaps I will let it in, begin to feel the space where
my heart is broken,
Seldom spoken.
This sorrow, yes, tomorrow.
More tears to be shed, more memories to tuck into a trunk,
More chocolate to consume, nothing to resolve by getting drunk.
This sorrow, yes, tomorrow.
I will feel you tomorrow, this sorrow.
Stay at a distance, just one more day
I will embrace you, your wisdom I will borrow
Tomorrow, welcome sorrow.

Do not wait for tomorrow – just for today…

… let the Spirit of Sorrow have you.

DAY 130

Be Inspired

TODAY: the first day of an inspired, inspirited life.

What is in you that is calling itself forth?

Are you restless? Are you feeling there is always something else?

Is there fire in your belly?

Do not be afraid to speak and act on these feelings.
Do not be afraid of your dreams.
Do not be afraid of asking someone else to help you achieve them.

Inspiration is contagious.

Just for today...

... let the Spirit of Inspiration have you.

DAY 131

Sorrow

Some days the sorrow is too great to bear
I see and hear her everywhere
Her blessings became a burden
She did not know we knew or cared

Some days the sorrow is a window into the past
We weep for all that was
And all that could not last

Some days the sorrow is a blessing
A reminder of the pain, knowing a love so great
Is a gift from spirit below and above

Some days the sorrow is a passage
Into the suffering of others
That we are not alone
The path is lined with silver
A cord leading us home.

Some days the sorrow
Allows her to visit, her message
"I was with you before I was born,
I am with you now, will be with you
To birth your soul when you return."

Until tomorrow, no more sorrow.

Just for today...

... let the Spirit of Collective Sorrow have you.

DAY 132

Negativity

Any issue, negativity, problem, pessimism, is never external. It is always internal.

Find out today what is really going on inside you.

Why are you seething? What is in you that needs an adjustment?

Do a chakra scan; ask your soul where you need pay attention. Is your back hurting? Maybe there is trouble in your marriage or your finances. Is your throat bothering you? Maybe you need to speak out loud to someone about some issue.

Seek and you shall find.

Just for today...

... let Spirit have you.

DAY 133

Angel of Light

Do not allow the angel of light to dim in you.

Love unconditionally.

Choose forgiveness,

Be hopeful,

Be in unity,

Seek peace,

Have compassion.

Just for today...

... allow the Spirit of Angel Light to have you.

DAY 134

The Spirit of the Departed

To honour those who have passed, live your best life. Grieve with passion, let go, live like no one is watching, dance for those who have left us and honour them with your life. Serve, be kind, forgive, live completely.

Just for today…

… let the Spirit of Those Who Have Departed have you.

DAY 135

The Spirit of the Dance

As he took her in his arms to dance their favourite dance,
Giggles passed through her lips, now this dance fits.

The dance of life, oh this is fine
The dance of the Divine
Is flowing through her.

Just for today...

... Dance with the Divine.

DAY 136

Live Your Life Purpose

LIVE YOUR LIFE PURPOSE.

Love your life on purpose.

Live your life with purpose.

You will have a Purpose for your Life.

Just for today...

... let the Purpose of Your Life have you.

DAY 137

Out of My Mind

"I am out of my mind," you say.

"Did you lose it?" I ask.

"No," you reply, "I am into my heart and I love it."

Good, you have found yourself. You have found your spiritual gold.

Being out of your mind is freeing. No attachments.

Just for today...

... let the Spirit of Losing Your Mind and Finding Your Heart have you.

DAY 138

The Spirit of Chaos

There is a divine order to what we consider chaos.
There is an order we cannot see.
We must trust, let go and continue to BE.
If you feel yourself spinning, relax and start singing!

Just for today...

... let the Spirit of Divine Chaos have you.

DAY 139

The Spirit of Attitude

Another day. Oh God, noooo...

or

OH GOD, another day! Yippee!!

Attitude.

Just for today...

...let the Spirit of Adjusting Your Attitude have you.

DAY 140

Ego Be Still

Living my dream, or dreaming my life?
Whatever it is, it's feeling alright.
Day to day, praying and playing, I can see over the hill.
Handing my day over, not following my will,
Let Spirit have me. EGO, be still.

Just for today...

... let Spirit have you.

DAY 141

The True Spirit of EGO

You do not need ego behind you, following.

You do not need ego in front, leading you.

You need ego beside you, in harmony, to balance mind, body and spirit.

Just for today…

… embrace ego with grace and allow the true Spirit of Ego to have you.

DAY 142

The Spirit of Freedom

A few years ago someone told me that no one would take me seriously in the business world as I was such a free spirit.

They did not know who they were taking to, as I had been working in the business world since I had been a wee one.

They also did not know that a free spirit is a free spirit and can do all things freely.

Just for today...

... let the Freedom of Your Free Spirit have you.

DAY 143

The Spirit of Waking Up

When our daughter Melanie took her own life in May, I received a call from my mentor and teacher, Caroline. Her message was most welcome that day, as we were on our way to Melanie's funeral and I was not finding any "fun" in "funeral" — especially this one.

Her comment to me was: "Lilly, this grief is not yours alone — it belongs to the collective." Okay, I felt that in my body; that helped me get through the day. But my mind was still in shock and I just did not understand. Within months I came to an understanding of the collective consciousness of the whole.

I have had a relaxation tool in my practice since 2001 — the Trinity Table. The 500-pound table of solid oak slowly spins (four turns per minute), putting your mind into a theta state (as achieved in deep sleep) that allows you to relax, breathing in comfort. Your experience is whatever your intention is.

On one of my personal rides, my intention was to be with Melanie and feel her. The ride started in its usual way — with deep relaxation, into sleep — when suddenly I felt her. Her message was brief but centuries-long in nature. "Mom, I was with you before I was born, I was with you as you mothered me for thirty-seven years, and I will be with you when I mother your soul into the collective."

Alert now, I stopped the table. And I understood what Caroline had told me. I also realized that there is a deep "hole in the whole." What does this mean? Let me try to explain.

We need to take ownership of everything that happens to us. We all know that, right? That means if I am bullied, chances are I will bully. If I say something negative about someone, I say it for everyone. Everyone at some point will feel it. It is that universal truth: What goes around, comes around. We think we are off the hook, that this does not concern us; but wake up — there is a hole in the whole. That hole is you, your thoughts, your actions. If you think and feel they do not make a difference, open your eyes, your heart — they do.

I take ownership for my daughter's suicide. I do not blame myself, but I had a great part in her unhappiness. There were many things said and done, and I could have reacted differently. In some ways Melanie never had a chance at happiness. I won't go into the details, but that is a truth. I could have fought with the doctors years ago — I knew there was something wrong. Mental illness is raw. When the doctors said there was nothing wrong with her, who was I to argue? I was her mother; I needed to fight for her to give her a chance. Maybe because I own that now, other mothers are sensing this and changing, allowing their children to feel secure, loved, nurtured, whole. If something is not right with your child, find out why, listen to your heart, not your head or the doctors; keep fighting for their right to live a normal life.

Making choices, the right choices, means everything. We choose how to love, when to love, and whom to love. That is not a silly statement, but NOT understanding the implications of it IS. If we are to choose love, then Baby, buckle up. It means love those who speak poorly of you. Love those who beat you, blame you, left you. I am not saying you need to accept their actions, but if you are to choose love, then learn to forgive — love them anyway.

Yes, I am being judgmental right now and not contributing to the collective with love. I am trying to make a point.

Those who do not believe in the dark night of the soul have not suffered enough. Their time is up. The dark night does not come from ego. It is a passage into wholeness. For some it may not be in this lifetime. It can take many lifetimes. A collection of lifetimes. A dark night is holy; it is whole.

Watch and listen to a child for an hour living in their truth (not from a book they read); now they are inspiring.

Trust me, I have been there; I have been one of those people who thought to make a difference. I have been on the receiving end of Midas/Miser archetypes — of negativity and jealousy. Letting go; letting God. Goddess is a gift from the spirit of our collective. Letting Spirit have me, surrendering has its blessings.

These words are not to inspire you; that's Spirit's work. My hope is that they wake you up; that you realize you may be the hole in the whole and can fill up this collective consciousness with love, acceptance, unity, peace, forgiveness and compassion. You came from it and will return to it. You are that.

Just for today…

…Wake Up to the Hole in the Whole.

DAY 144

The Spirit of Belief

I BELIEVE.

It can be a belief in your creativity, your employees or your employers. It can be a belief in something bigger than yourself. It can be a belief in yourself. A belief in now, the sacred, whatever you believe in.

Make it BIG... BEAUTIFUL, BLISSFUL!

BELIEVE.

Just for today...

... let the Spirit of Belief have you.

DAY 145

The Spirit of Forgiveness

I went to the Garden of Eden today and there
I found a dream.

It did not belong to anyone but everyone who lived with love,
hope and forgiveness as their theme.

Just for today...

... let the Spirit of Forgiveness have you.

DAY 146

The Spirit of Soul Healing

The needs of the soul to heal are very different from the needs of the body, ego or psyche.

Heal your soul through understanding the organs of the soul — your seven chakras. Visualize your root chakra, the colour red; your sacral chakra, orange; your solar plexus chakra, yellow; your heart chakra, green; your throat chakra, cobalt blue; your third eye, indigo; and your crown, violet. Make a daily practice of breathing into each chakra, visualizing each colour, and giving thanks that they are in harmony, vibrating in perfect unison with the universe.

Just for today...

... let the Spirit of Soul Healing have you.

DAY 147

The Spirit of Enough

I have all I need today

All is in harmony and chaos

Regret and acceptance

Light and shadow.

As the lily, it grows in the darkness of mud to reach the light of the sun, and blooms in beauty and balance.

It is and has enough.

I am filled with ENOUGH.

Just for today...

... let the Spirit of Enough have you.

DAY 148

The Spirit of Jeans

Girl, there is nothing as comfortable or holy than a good pair of jeans — jeans that fit around your bottom in the most loving, lovely places.

There is a pair of jeans out there for each of us; I do not care what age we are, what size we are. When we put on jeans, we feel young, alive and together.

Wear a pair of your favourite jeans today. If they do not fit, go buy another pair; the old ones will fit someone else.

Just be you in the best-fitting jeans,
made for your goddess body.

Just for today...

... let the Spirit of the Everyday Wisdom of Denim have you.

DAY 149

The Spirit of Acceptance

In that last moment when your heart stopped,
Your spirit freed you to join your soul, the collective soul.
In that moment you are everywhere but here, and I weep.
I weep with joy for your reunion with self,
with God and Goodness.
I weep for our loss, your vanilla smell, your radiant smile,
your creative self.
Yet, in gratitude, I bow on bended knee that you exist,
before, now and forever. Amen.

Just for today…

… let the Spirit of Acceptance of the Loss of a Loved One have you.

DAY 150

The Spirit of Light

Today, as you are embracing the energy of miracles,
Be conscious of your intent.
Allow the light to flow through you.

Awake to the light.

Feel the shift beginning to take place in you.

Just for today...

... let the Spirit of Miracles have you.

DAY 151

The Spirit of a Hug

A hug a day keeps the darkness away.

Today hug all whom you see and think about.

If not in the actual physical way, then hug what is ethereal. You will be hugging all of you.

If you are unable to hug for fear of rejection, hug in your mind; allow yourself to imagine that hug — either giving one or receiving one.

Now go pass that hug on.

Just for today…

… let the Spirit of Hugs have you.

DAY 152

The Spirit of Matter

There are things that matter and then there is the matter of THINGS.

Let go of these things that do not matter.

In your final moments, THINGS will not matter.

Just for today…

… let the Spirit of What Really Matters have you.

DAY 153

The Spirit of Stillness

Be still, for God's sake.

For God's sake you will feel the stillness of the Divine.

In stillness, your body slows down, your heart rate lowers,

Your blood flow relaxes, your mind clears,

Your heart and solar plexus open to receive.

In stillness, this is where the depth of the Divine resides.

Just for today…

… let the Spirit of Stillness have you.

DAY 154

The Spirit of Passion

Can you be loved and lose your love?
Can you be passionate and lose your passion?
"No," my passionate beloved replied.
"You were born in passionate love
And the love of your passion will never die;
It will only be transformed."

Just for today...

... let the Love of Your Passion have you.

DAY 155

The Spirit of Prayer

PRAYER, our Portal to Peace.

There is an energy that happens when we take our time to pray.

There is a doorway that opens, and, as we enter, let us be conscious of the details, the light flowing through us.

We do make a difference.

Prayer is the way to speak to the collective with the help of our guardians, guides, angels.

Just for today...

... let the Spirit of Prayer have you.

DAY 156

The Spirit of Emotions

Have you wondered where the fear went when you filled your heart with sentiment?

When we change our attitude or view about an opinion of something or someone, we change.

We see and feel both sides.

This is the key to releasing fear.

Hand it over and see, feel through the energy of Divine Source.

Open your heart today, see everyone and everything as they are, not as you want them to be.

Just for today…

… allow the Spirit of Your Emotions to flow.

DAY 157

The Spirit of Rain

RAIN, I love you. You nourish our gardens,
our plants, and our trees.
The birds and animals can drink freely, play in the breeze.
As your moisture hits the ground,
I will dance, around and around.
You cleanse the planet, whitewash anew.
When you are finished, I have a song for you.

Write your own song when it rains.
Sometimes we only want the sun on our backs, but rain is very important to our survival. It fills the planet up with goodness so we can reap the benefits.

Just for today…

… let the Spirit of the Nourishment of the Rain have you.

DAY 158

The Spirit of Your Journey

And the day came when the journey did not seem so long; when the longing was to journey inward.

One of the best tools for a journey is a pencil and a piece of paper.

Start writing, journaling.

You will go places, see things, feel alive, visit your subconscious mind.

When you unpack, you will note that the journal took you on a journey only you would understand.

Just for today…

… let the Spirit of YOUR Journey have you.

DAY 159

The Spirit of Change

Nothing changes unless you will it to change.

You will pray for change, long for change.

Unless you are able to do the work required,

Nothing changes.

Nothing changes when nothing changes.

If you live in fear of this change, Spirit will step in and change it for you, but not in the way you envisioned.

Now is a good time to make an assessment of your goals.

What is possible, what is manageable, what is a dream?

Be prepared to tweak and squeeze all that goodness out of you.

Just for today…

… let the Spirit of Change have you.

DAY 160

The Spirit of the Divine Dark Night

The Divine Dark Night — once you experience it, you can never return to what was.

Your soul will guide you.

Follow gracefully. A dark night is different for everyone; do not compare.

Allow the lessons in your darkness to have you. Flow with it. Shine your light on it so that it becomes a beacon to the hearth of your soul.

Do not be afraid, be aware.

Just for today...

...let the Spirit of Your Dark Night have you.

DAY 161

Reflections

Everyone, everything, everywhere is a reflection.
What is outside is IN.

Ponder this for a minute.

Envision what you are manifesting today. Reflect on who you want to be with, where you want to be. Whom do you best serve today?

Now go about your day with this image.

Before you know it, your life will reflect what you envisioned.

Just for today...

... let the Spirit of Your Reflection have you.

DAY 162

The Spirit of Obstacles

There are no obstacles, only opportunities to grow.
Sometimes we are blinded by a hurdle or block that is stopping our spirit's progress.
Do not allow anything or anyone to hinder this progress.
It is between you and the spirit of who you are.
Earlier we said you are a co-creator. Bring out your inner warrior.
Build a new pathway to your growth. Not in a bitter, angry fashion, but with grace, dignity and compassion.

Just for today...

... let the Spirit of Your Inner Warrior remove your obstacles.

DAY 163

The Spirit of Goodness

When we see the Good in ourselves, we will see the Good in others; we will learn to live with non-judgment; we will come to understand we are all one, in Goodness, in God, in Goddess.

Just for today…

… let the Spirit of Your Goodness have you.

DAY 164

The Spirit of Exercise

Just as your body, your spirituality needs to be stretched and strengthened daily, so...

build your altar and pray daily

find a yoga centre

journal daily

eat alive foods grown locally

volunteer

light a candle for someone in need

see a health therapist

go to an angel workshop

be where you are, instead of wishing your life away

Just for today...

... let the Spirit of Your Daily Spiritual Exercises have you.

DAY 165

The Spirit of Decisions

You make decisions hourly, daily.

When you make a decision, you need to devote your energies only to that choice.

You do not need to fear making decisions. The moment you make them, the timing is right for that moment.
Allow Spirit to guide you.

Just for today…

… let the Spirit of Your Decisions have you.

DAY 166

The Spirit of Sharing

What is spiritual sharing? Do we share because it makes us feel good? Are we not feeding our EGOs?

Spiritual sharing is sharing even when is it uncomfortable for us. For example, we're not sharing spiritually if we withhold compliments about someone's good deeds because we have an issue with that person.

Spiritual sharing brings many blessings into our lives. We may not even be aware of them.

The more uncomfortable it is for us, the more our souls evolve.

Just for today...

... let the Spirit of Unconditional Sharing have you.

DAY 167

The Spirit of Magic

I thought I needed a magic wand,
When at once I realized
The magic, I had it all along.

Just for today…

… let the Spirit of Your Inner Magician have you.

DAY 168

A Day of Happy

Focus on a day of Happy today.

Awake happy to be alive; happy for the vehicle you will ride or drive —it can be a bicycle, a car, a motorcycle, a trolley, a bus.

Happy to see someone.

Happy there is so much beauty in the world.

Happy to see your reflection as you wash or shave your face.

Happy for the clean water you wash in.

Happy for the strength to walk through a day filled with grace.

Happy for true friendships.

If you are plump, happy for your plumpness, for you are thankful for your food.

Happy for every WOW you will embrace today.

Happy for your grief, for you experienced deep love.

Happy you are living and loving it.

Just for today…

… let the Spirit of Happy have you.

DAY 169

The Spirit of Feelings

It's okay not to be okay.
No matter what you are feeling, live your truth.
Tomorrow is another day. Feelings, like the tides
Come and go. Allow the flow.

Just for today…

… let the Spirit of Your Feelings have you.

DAY 170

The Spirit of Our Silent Walk

A rhythm is set as we take our first step
a walk is needed this first day of summer
silently we put one foot in front of the other
no words are needed after years of loving one another

We are in our own thoughts
about a child we just lost
a yellow butterfly plays and sways around our feet
slowly rises above our heads
my heart, it skips a beat

for just one moment in time
she is with us and we are able to find

her image, her image is not our imagination
the light of her is clear
she is free, to be, to be
in silence, her flight, our walk
our walk in sacred silence

Just for today...
... let your Silent Walk have you;
believe in what you cannot see.

DAY 171

The Spirit of Sacred Time

There are times in our lives when we become derailed from our destiny, especially in times of trauma or challenge.

We must remember the blessings and realize that we do not have to live in linear time, and can breathe into the realm of the infinite — in sacred time.

In sacred time we feel joy and our healing is birthed. It is normal to feel joy when all in our life is joy-filled, but to BE joy, feel joy, when we are in challenges — this is sacred. This is the whole of the holy. We must be gentle with ourselves and others.

Just for today...

... let the Spirit of Your Challenges and Your Joys have you.

DAY 172

Summer

Summer is officially here. Feel the pulse of the Earth.

Feel the aliveness, the awe of life.

Plant something today and watch it grow. On the first day of summer I usually like to plant lavender — the symbolism of yin-yang, all in perfect balance:

- Spiritual healing
- Tranquility
- Higher consciousness
- Release of energy blockages
- Easing of tension
- Promotion of calmness
- Purification

The fullness of everything alive and in healing.

Just for today…

… let the Spirit of Summer have you.

DAY 173

The Spirit of Summer

Summer begins in the Northern Hemisphere when it is tilted most directly toward the sun and the daylight lingers the longest. It has always been my favourite time of the year.

Journal your desires today. Put them away until next year's first day of summer.

When you reread your journal next year, you will discover that most of what you had written came to pass.

See, you had it all along.

Just for today...

... let the Spirit of Summer have you.

DAY 174

The Spirit of Your Genius

Why did you come to Earth?

Are you excited to have your genius give birth to your greatest self?

Allow your creative and natural ability to flow, to erupt in you. You are original, you are brilliant, you carry wisdom passed down through the ages.

I ask you again, why did you come to Earth?

Make notes today on this question.

Just for today…

… let the Spirit of Your Genius have you.

DAY 175

The Spirit of Fairy Day

This is Fairy Day.

A day to believe in magic,

The unknown,

The possibilities,

The what-ifs.

Free your mind from judgments and allow the magic to return.

Just for today…

… let the fairies have you.

DAY 176

The Dance of Joy

Upon my daily ritual of walking through the rice fields here at Puri Taman Sari, I am in rhythm with the dance. There are butterflies — many variations as far as the eye can see — making romance.

They dance in harmony, in their joy — who knows if it's a girl or a boy. They are just being. They jive around a frangipani tree, foxtrot their way intensely.

At the speed of the eternal, internal Om, they samba on their own to the sound of the drum.

Together flying around, they spin into a waltz.

I watch, awestruck, as they perform my favourite, the cha-cha, and then, alas, they fly off with the speed of shooting stars.

I am left holding my breath, for once again the universe has spoken words of wisdom: Be in rhythm, step lightly, stand tall, dance your life with joy. Give it your ALL.

Just for today...

... let the Spirit of Your Dance have you.

DAY 177

The Spirit of Generosity

When you really want something and get it,
And know it will give others pleasure,
GIVE IT AWAY.

Just for today…

… let the Energy of Generosity have you.

DAY 178

The Spirit of Surrender

If you cannot find strength and are lying on your back, that's the time to surrender, AGAIN.

Sometimes we need to be physically sick and on our backs in total surrender to understand just how fragile we really are; to appreciate that we live in the third dimensional space. Earth is a wonderful place/space to be. We do not need to be anywhere else but here. NOW.

Just for today...

... let the Spirit of Total Surrender have you.

DAY 179

The Spirit of YOU

You are not alone.

You are loved because you exist.

You are loved because you are loving.

You are loved because you ARE YOU.

Just for today...

... let the love of Spirit have you.

DAY 180

The Spirit of Friendship

Friendships are mirrors — inner reflections.

Friends help each other feel good and challenge one another to be their best.

How about the friends who teach us lessons we don't necessarily want to learn? The ones who take and never give? The ones who use us for their own development? The ones who talk about us when our back is turned?

These noble friends — remember, we choose them and they are here to teach us more about ourselves.

Love them anyway.

Just for today...

... let the true Spirit of Noble Friendship have you.

DAY 181

The Spirit of Colour

I dreamt I was a rainbow, colours to behold.
With every breath I took
The colours turned to gold.
The gold was lustrous and shiny
As pure as divine light
The wealth of who I am is bold,
Beautiful and bright.

See yourself as this light today. If you are unable to envision, allow the rainbow of a prism to flow through you.

Just for today...

... let your inner GOLD shine.

DAY 182

Fate

Are you fated to live your destiny or are you fated to change your destiny?

Take charge today and LIVE your destiny, your dreams, your desires.

Remember we are here to serve, not to get what we deserve.

Live your life with hope, peace, compassion, unity and love.

Just for today...

... let the Spirit of Your Destiny guide you.

DAY 183

The Spirit of Death

"Death," she said, "what are you talking about?

You are all asleep, and once you wake, you will come to realize that death is simply a birth to Beauty, Love and Divine Order, the likes of which you can only imagine.

When we meet again, we will rejoice in the spirit of this Love, Beauty and Divine."

"Ah," I replied, "yes, I think I remember. Thank you, Darling... until we meet again."

Just for today...

... let the Spirit of Dying to Wake Up have you.

DAY 184

Your Mountain

There will always be a mountain to climb;
A personal goal or just growing old.
We will climb to the top only to find our way down.
We look around and begin the climb once more,
but not like before.
This time it is easier and we glide with ease
as we take others with us, if they so please.
We will each reach heights of our highest potential; our
personal destiny.
We become one in our efforts, that moment feels like eternity.

Just for today...

...let the Spirit of Your Challenge have you; and know that in this challenge you are not alone.

DAY 185

The Spirit of Change

Are you a better person today than you were yesterday?

Are you more at peace, more in love with life, more giving, more patient?

You have the opportunity to change, one day at a time.

Just for today…

… let the Spirit of Change have you.

DAY 186

The Spirit of Freedom

Born Free, Live Free, BE Free, in your mind, body and spirit.

Take the liberty to be YOU today.

You are not in bondage or slavery.

If you are, it is of your own making. Break the ties that bind you. Ask for help if needed.

Just for today...

... let the Spirit of Freedom have you,

and feel gratitude for that freedom.

DAY 187

Dig Deeper

"Take me down Lord to the reason I was born."
— Caroline Myss

Just when you think you can't dig deeper, love more, serve more, laugh louder, dream bigger... you find out you CAN...

Because just for today...

... you let Spirit have you.

DAY 188

The Spirit of Birthdays

Celebrate a birthday.

I love birthdays, whether they're my own, a family member's, or a friend's. It doesn't matter how old we are when we are celebrating someone — we are rejoicing and saying, "I am happy you are alive."

Have you ever noticed that at funerals we appraise, applaud, and celebrate the life of the deceased? I believe this to be a lovely gesture, but imagine if that person heard our joy-filled praise yearly... they could enjoy their joy.

For birthdays I fuss; I bake. I make or purchase a small gift — a token. I am never embarrassed about the giving. Nor am I ashamed to receive. We have Santa Claus at Christmas, and I believe we have "because you exist" helpers at birthdays.

Do you know of an upcoming birthday? Celebrate! Is it your birthday? Allow others to tell you how they appreciate you. Enjoy the fuss. Don't wait until you are not around to hear your name sung in the spirit of love. You are here NOW.

Just for today...

...let the Spirit of Celebrating Birthdays have you.

DAY 189

The Spirit of Archetypes

"Every accident precedes a loss of power." Wise words from a good friend of mine and spiritual adviser, Jim C.

(If you have studied with Caroline Myss or taken my archetype class at Whitelight, you have an understanding of archetypes that will help you understand today's tale.)

I have the Thief archetype in my eighth house; she hides until I confront her. I am not a thief who will take something from you, but I will steal your time or your sense of worth if you are not strong enough to resist.

Speaking of reacting, I had the most interesting day yesterday. I had been talking about taking quality time off to reenergize. Since April of last year, when I opened the White Lilly clothes shop, time alone has been a wee bit difficult to find. Yes, I make it that way. I am way ahead of you, your thoughts, remember?

Anyway, I happened to be in the doctor's office when she spoke about my inability to relax. Not a big deal unless you are teaching others to relax and not taking your own advice. When I was back at Whitelight, thinking of this, I felt this push from behind, tripped, and down I went, full face without grace on the cement floor. Stunned, I picked myself up, picked up broken glass, and sat down in silence for a few minutes.

Nothing hurt except everything, so I felt fine. Yes, Spirit, I got the message: Relax or I will be pushed into it. Indeed, I fractured my arm in that fall. But back to what I wanted to tell you about the Thief.

After the fall, I was still in shock, when I went into the White Lilly. I was told that a client had been on Facebook telling about how she came into the store and fit herself with Goddess on the Go (the line of clothing from Bali, sold in Canada only at my shop at the time), but instead of buying from us or asking us to order a specific colour and size for her, she placed an order online directly to the manufacturer. I was horrified. Perhaps it was because I was still hurting from my fall, but this felt like an emotional hurt.

How can someone who knows how we pride ourselves in the beautiful energy of our store environment come in, get her size, then order elsewhere? I felt violated, as if someone had come in and stolen something from me.

Wounded me (woe to the Victim archetype), witnessing my thoughts, I changed.

I FELT, I KNEW, that no one could take anything from me. This is a free country we live in; she can shop anywhere in the world. She can use me, I can be hurt, but only if I choose to be. I came to an understanding that she had no idea what it took to find this line of clothing, to open this business. She had no idea what efforts I had gone through to select and co-design the clothing, as well as opening and running my shop.

Now I am free to love this woman who reflects my own Thief. I am also free to say, "No, you cannot continue to come into my store and use my energy or my staff's time to help you order our product elsewhere." I am not that evolved... yet!

What does all this have to do with my fall? Sometimes the universe pushes us into an energy field — a time to rest — so we can assess ourselves as we grow through our ascension process. Our archetypes take us to places of new discoveries. The Thief helps shine and direct you to your spiritual gold, our spiritual goals.

One of my goals has been to stop judging others even if I feel hurt by their actions. I want to go into the mirror and see their intentions. I hope to feel their intentions and come to an understanding that they are reflections of me.

We have all been ascending for a number of years (moving inward, upward, to our highest selves). Many of us chose to live consciously, and conscious living has hit us hard and hurts — emotionally, physically and spiritually.

For today, my wish for you is that you be aware, not afraid. Whatever your archetypes, embrace them. Embracing your archetypes, in light and shadow, leads you not into temptation but delivers you from your old self.

Just for today...

... let the Spirit of Your Archetypes have you.

DAY 190

Transform Yourself

When you find yourself feeling helpless or hopeless today, repeat to yourself:

"I can transform in an instant."

Put your reactive thoughts on hold and connect to a new energy that sets you free.

Just for today…

… let the Spirit of Your New Story have you.

DAY 191

The Spirit of Boundaries

At this time in our evolution we are being called and urged to expand our vision. The secret is getting over ourselves and learning to see others first and ourselves second. Only then will we develop the tools to rise above the five senses and tune in to our sixth sense.

We have become obsessed with "I"; I need to look after my feelings, my space, my thoughts. This is all from our intellect. When we move from our intellect, we make room to live from our heart, and the heart is in light, not the fight with I. We can then step out of our pain and feel the pain of a friend, partner, parent or child, and do something about it. I believe Jesus was teaching us symbolically when he died on the cross. It was never about him; it was about humanity. "Forgive them, they know not what they do."

I am not talking about letting someone walk over your boundaries, but really, can you step out of your personal pain and think of other people first? Hurt people hurt people. If someone is hurting you in some way, it is because that person is hurting. Can you step aside and love that person the way they are unable to love themselves? Look at this person without judgment.

Yes, I realize from my own experience that this is not always easy. I have days, hours, minutes, when I have to repeat, repeat: "Focus on this person's needs; yours are being taken care of because you allow Spirit to have you." Whether it involves their business, their family, their livelihood or their self-esteem, because they are loved enough they will come to think of others instead of themselves and pass it on.
This passing love on — isn't that where you and me become THEE?

We are co-creating, living in unity within our community to nourish mind, body, spirit. We have passed the energy of hurting ourselves by denying others love.

Just for today...

...let Spirit have you.

DAY
192

The Spirit of Energy Intelligence

Everything we do, say and act out has an energy intelligence. We have the power to bring in light or shadow.

What are you choosing today?

Power up your life by focusing on the light within to beam throughout.

Just for today...

... let the Spirit of Your Energy Intelligence have you.

DAY 193

The Spirit of Mistakes

Mistakes are just that — MISS TAKES — about what we are deciding or observing in that moment.

It might be right for that moment, but we change... everything around us changes, and when we realize this we move on, move forward, and make another decision.

Just for today...

... let the Spirit of Your Decisions have you;

for in the moment, they are in divine order.

DAY 194

The Spirit of Offerings

An offering, either on your altar at home or given to a family member or friend, is a thank-you note to the universe.

Offerings are not exchanges for something. You are giving unconditionally.

Just for today...

... let the Spirit of Giving Unconditionally have you.

DAY 195

The Spirit of Your Ancestors

ONLY YOU have the ability to transform your daily routines, your weekly hours, your monthly habits.

Allow the energy, the memories of your ancestors, come through. Their wisdom will help you transform into your highest potential.

Remember your ancestors; they will remind you of where you came from.

Just for today...

... let the Spirit of Your Ancestors have you.

DAY 196

The Spirit of Unraveling Your Truth

What is your truth?

If you have siblings in your household, chances are they each have their own truths, their own stories.

I know twin men who were recently reminiscing about their youth. Grant saw their stepfather as a tyrant who mistreated them and their mother. He has a deep-rooted wound and still speaks ill of this man sixty years later. Greg, on the other hand, remembers their stepfather as a disciplinarian rather than a tyrant, and never saw him physically abuse their mother, though he knew she was verbally mistreated. Same household – two very different perspectives.

What is interesting is that Greg is a very compassionate man with an exceptional ability to forgive. His truth is that everyone is who they are for a reason, and we have to walk in someone else's shoes to fully understand them. Greg lives with an empathic heart. Empathy is his truth; it is his habit; it is not a feeling that comes and goes depending on circumstances. He lives with compassion and empathy and passes them on to everyone he encounters.

Whatever these brothers' stories, they are their truth. They have become habit. I see it in how they live their daily lives.

What is your truth? Can you love completely without judgment or conditions? Can you give without reaching for something in return? What is the truth in your DNA? Are you always ill because it was habit when you were younger to seek attention when you were ill? Are you a bully because you made a habit of always defending yourself?

Unravel the truth you tell yourself and take responsibility for it. Become aware, but never afraid. Your truth will set you free.

Just for today…

…let the Spirit of Unravelling Your Truth have you.

DAY 197

The Spirit of How to Power Up Your Life

Give life to the power within you.
Ignite your inner fire once again.
Be compassion, love, hope, peace, unity.
Now go serve that up for others to embrace.

Just for today...

... let Spirit have you.

DAY 198

The Spirit of Fear

There are days when a fear feels like we are walking a high wire.

I have come to understand that if we focus inward and know we are living our destiny and are not fated to our fear — if we KNOW that Spirit is guiding us — we can walk peacefully through that fear.

Just for today...

...let the Spirit of Your Fear, Your Focus Inward, have you.

DAY 199

The Spirit of Mandela

Mandela's birthday, July 18th, has been designated by the U.N. as Nelson Mandela International Day. In celebration of Mr. Mandela's life and legacy, we can serve as catalysts for each and every person. The U.N. joined a call by the Nelson Mandela Foundation to devote sixty-seven minutes of time to helping others to represent the sixty-seven years Mandela himself devoted to the service of humanity.

We realize that we have the ability to change the world through action.

Just for today...

... let the Spirit of Action have you.

DAY 200

The Spirit of Your Truth

Live your TRUTH, follow your TRUTH, even when the world is in denial of what you know to be true.

PS: I am thinking of journalist David Walsh and his truth about Lance Armstrong, and how everyone was in denial for a while. Yes, truth always prevails.

Just for today…

… let the Spirit of Your Truth have you.

DAY 201

The Spirit of Sunday

I see a yellow bird on the wire. Suddenly I am filled with an inner fire to live this day, Sunday, with joy and passion.

Thank you, yellow bird. The sun may not be shining, but it is there.

Just for today…

… let the Spirit of the SUN in Sunday have you.

DAY 202

The Spirit of Your Reality

Your reality comes from deep within you.

To create or change your world,

Love endlessly,

Pray daily,

Give unconditionally,

Serve as if no one is watching.

Just for today...

... let the Spirit of Your Reality lead you.

DAY 203

The Spirit of Acceptance

There will be days when everything in your life looks hazy;
Days when you feel hopeless and lazy.
There will be upsetting news from afar;
It will all seem bizarre,
But alas,
This too shall pass,
And you will remember.

Just for today…

… let the Spirit of Acceptance have you.

DAY 204

The Spirit of Healing

All is forgotten, all is forgiven, all is all loving.

True healing is difficult if you do not practice and apply: forget, forgive, love.

Just for today...

... let the Spirit of Healing have you.

DAY 205

The Spirit of a Recipe

Recipe of the day: a heart filled with love.
A drop of mindfulness,
An ounce of compassion,
A cup of joy.
Let it simmer while you are in prayer or meditation.
Let it rise up and share it with others.

Just for today…

… let the Spirit of Your Creation have you.

DAY 206

The Spirit of Your Inside Job

Stop waiting for and wanting someone to fix you — it's an inside job.

Sometimes we are just plain lazy; we fall into habits that are not good for us.

We have come a long way together, you and I, these last few months. By now you realize that your freedom is an inside job. Find the key or the combination.

You might have to go to a spiritual director, but remember that they cannot take out or pull out what is inside you. That is an inside job.

Just for today...

... let the Spirit of Your Inner Self have you.

DAY 207

The Spirit of Acceptance

Today you may be praying for your neighbour, mother, father, son-in-law — all going

through adversity at this time.

Operations, illness, chemo, heart issues, strokes. Life and death — a fine balance.

Praying for the outcome you want is not prayer. It is asking for Santa Claus. It is asking to get what you want.

Prayer is helping the universe align with the destiny of those you pray for. It is a power surge. Prayer is acknowledging their fate and Spirit's will for them. This is acceptance.

It is the fighting spirit within them wanting another day, month, year.

We all bargain with the God of our understanding.
The outcome may very well be as we request, not because we or they are favoured, but because that is their destiny.

Pray, Pray. Pray, love filled with grace.

Invoke healing and acceptance. If the outcome is in alignment with your request, rejoice and give thanks.

Gratitude, another form of Prayer. Let go; let GOD.

Just for today…

…let us pray for the Spirit of Acceptance.

DAY 208

The Spirit of Embracing Self

No matter our past, it does not last.

In this moment we can reinvent ourselves.

Just for today, let the Spirit of Being the Person You Always Wanted to Be have you.

If you want to change, be the change.

If you are happy with who you are, EMBRACE yourself and others will follow your lead.

Just for today…

…let the Spirit of Embracing Self have you.

DAY 209

The Spirit of Blessings

Today, I say "Good morning" or "Hello" to you.
It is be a blessing of hope,
A blessing of love.

I see you and acknowledge your existence.
How blessed we are to be together on this planet
at the same time.

We are not getting off this planet alive,
So enjoy the day, this moment,
And bless all whom you meet today with a simple
"Hello, halo."

Just for today...

... let the Spirit of Blessings have you.

Did you remember to download your free *Power Up Your Life 30-Day Challenge Workbook?* I hope it will be a blessing to you.

Your copy awaits at www.powerupyourlife.com/readergift

DAY 210

The Spirit of If

If I were a snake,
I'd swim in the lake
And swim my emotions away.

If I were a canary,
I'd find a fairy
And fly to a mystical place and stay.

But I am ME,
I am happy to see,
So I will embrace this day
With joy and glee.

Just for today…

… let the Spirit of Your Humanness have you.

DAY 211

The Spirit of Today

Today I am going to feel everything as if for the first time.
Yesterday it was people, places and things outside of me.
The discovery.
Today it is about me. I will feel my emotions with wonder. I will my will to not take things personally.
I will pay attention to the song in my heart,
To the rhythm in my step,
To the call of my soul.
I will watch myself as I witness my bravery, my vulnerability.

Just for today...

... let the Spirit of Your Inner Witness have you.

DAY 212

The Spirit of Wonder

Live today as if it is your last.

Really taste your first cup of coffee.

Look into your beloved's eyes before you say goodbye with longing for their return.

Enter your day with awe and wonder.

Embrace whatever, chaos or order, with amazement and play.

Start seeing, feeling, hearing, sensing, as if for the first time.

Just for today...

... let the Spirit of Wonder have you.

DAY 213

The Spirit of Possibilities

Be open to all possibilities.

Be open to non-judgment.

You never know what or whom the universe will bring to you this day.

Fill in the blank: "WHAT IF _______________?"

Now wait, watch, celebrate.

Just for today...

... let the Spirit of Possibilities have you.

DAY 214

The Spirit of Choices

FATE is the mirage; DESTINY is the miracle.

What does fate have in store for you? What do the stars tell you? What is predetermined for you in this lifetime?

The choices you make change your fate,
so you live your destiny.

It is not what happens to you; it is what you do
with what happens.

Just for today…

… let the Spirit of Choices have you.

DAY 215

The Spirit of Adventure

Pack for an adventure today.

Pack light, for you need nothing but you. Do not worry or stress about the things you cannot change, but change the things you can.

Pray that you accept any outcome on this journey. You have done all you can and it is now in Spirit's hands.

Just for today...

... let the Spirit of Adventure have you.

DAY 216

The Spirit of Daily Rituals

Daily rituals become habits.

Meditation, yoga, prayer, conscious moments you are aware of, grace/blessings before eating, and walking are a few examples.

What are your daily rituals? Write them down — you will be surprised by how many you actually have.

Honour your personal rituals, for they are yours alone and are sacred.

Just for today…

… let the Spirit of Your Daily Rituals have you.

DAY 217

The Spirit of Your Story

Your story is a joyous reunion of your mind, body and spirit. You do not need to change your story when you learn to look through the lens of symbolism. It is an amazing story; one of living your highest potential. A story mixed with pleasure, pain, grief, joy, wisdom, learning, love, forgetfulness, awakenings and so much more.

Do not be ashamed of your story. Honour your history, your ancestors.

Now go — write or tell your story. Not from the Wounded Child, but from the Divine or Magical Child.

Just for today...

... let the Spirit of Your Story have you.

DAY 218

The Spirit of Release

To have and to hold is hoarding.
To release and be bold,
Let go of control;
That is how your story is told.

Just for today…

…Release, AGAIN!

DAY 219

The Spirit of Clutter

I was in a slump, felt like I was in the dumps
I had so much clutter and more

I had baggage galore, like never before
It took days to sort, there was nothing left to preserve
But I did not mind, I knew it was time to let go of all
that did not serve

I kicked out any thoughts that were holding me back
And opened my heart to light
Then I began on my living space
And swept out the cobwebs without haste

Today, where does your clutter lie?
Is it taking up room in your head or your living quarters?
There is a sense of freedom when we de-clutter

Just for today...

... let the Spirit of Decluttering have you.

DAY 220

The Spirit of Knowing Why

It is said that you cannot move forward from something unless you walk through it. Sometimes it's okay to want to know the "why" of things; to come to an understanding and finally the freedom of acceptance.

Why does a fifty-year-old suddenly tattoo their body from head to toe, becoming a rebel with a cause?

Why is it okay for society or a family to think that casual sex at twelve, thirteen, fourteen or fifteen years of age is okay? And to give these youths condoms to carry in batches in their handbags or pockets? And to have their doctors give them drugs for anxiety?

Why do we think it is okay to have someone from another country raise our children while that person's children are without a parent?

We need to see everything symbolically and understand the language of the twelve houses, twelve archetypes, through sacred contracts. It answers the WHY and, in my opinion, there is only one answer. Do you know it? Once you do, acceptance can bring you peace.

Just for today...

...let the Spirit of Knowing Why have you.

DAY 221

The Spirit of Meditation

There is a space only you can visit. Go inside this multidimensional depth often.

Pray, play.

Return full, free and ready to live your destiny.

Just for today…

… let the Spirit of Meditation have you.

DAY 222

The Spirit of Another Tomorrow

I am trying, but I cannot stop crying

The losses are too great, you know

It is difficult not to show

The human side of us

For we desire our spirit to flow

And it does, just not the way we had hoped

The Divine is with us as we cope

It is up to us to shield ourselves from the shadow

That seeps through us as sorrow

But for tomorrow, there is always tomorrow

Just for today...

... believe in Tomorrow.

DAY 223

The Spirit of Your Vision

Keep your vision alive.

Birth it into existence by breathing into the organs of your soul, your chakras.

Just for today...

... let the Spirit of Your Vision have you.

DAY 224

The Spirit of the Challenge

This is a day when stress seems to be unmanageable. Maybe your phone is not working or your network provider is down. Perhaps the car won't start, the fridge is on the fritz, your ATM card is lost. These are interesting times, and what stressed our parents is different from what we and our children stress over.

Let go, hang on, hang low, but don't hang up. I had a brother and a daughter who had days like this. They decided to hang it all up, themselves included. The residue left behind took years to rectify and added stress to the lives of their family members and future generations.

Let go; let God. This too shall pass, and you will regard today as just another day in the many days of your life. For every difficult day there are endless days of joy.

Hang on, hang low, but don't hang up.

Just for today...

...let the Spirit of the Challenge have you.

DAY 225

The Spirit of Dying to Be Awake

In 2005 I took a group to Bali on one of our Blissful Bali spiritual journeys. This trip was different right from the start.

My husband, John, was coming with me, as well as our daughter Amanda and her fiancé, Mark. Family, support. Yippee — this trip would be filled with enlightenment for all!

It started off well enough. Picked up at the airport by our spiritual family, Agung Prana and his son Wah, we settled in nicely without incident. There were fifteen of us in all, and we had just flown for twenty-four hours. We settled into our private villas, swam in our private pools, ate, and had a starry, dreamy night.

Next day we left for Taman Sari, a resort in one of my favourite places on the planet: North Bali. Coral reefs, fresh Balinese food, full moon, Balinese dancers. Mornings bring yoga on the beach, fresh fruit for breakfast, Balinese coffee, and a two-hour workshop on my work,

Manifesting the Magic in You (based on Caroline Myss's work with archetypes). The afternoons are filled with open spiritual discussions, swimming in the Bali Sea, massage or meditation. In the evenings we enjoy fresh fish, fresh fruit, and many more Balinese dishes made for our delight. Then it is off to temple for holy prayers. Beautiful colours, children playing, praying, baskets of offerings to the Gods. So much to see, feel and embrace.

After a few days we were on our way to Agung Prana's home, which houses many villas and a restaurant. Orchids everywhere you go, lilies the size of dinner plates and butterflies surrounding us — vivid colours everywhere. With wonder we watched the family and staff going about their lives in joy and bliss. There is no word in Balinese for "artist," as everything they do is with reverence and creativity; all is sacred.

One evening we all decided to have a channelling session. We sat in silence in the family temple with a priest and Mrs. Prana's sister as our channellers. After a few minutes of prayers the channelled began to make noises and scared a few in the group. Some in the group approached the channeller, sat with her and received messages from their relatives who had passed on. One young woman's mother came to her and wondered what she was dong in Bali. The channeller then began to sing to the young woman in English a lullaby that the woman's mother had sung to her when she was a child. The channeller did not speak English, so we knew this was the real deal. The group was transfixed.

I went to sit down next to the priest and immediately went into a trance. I went under, as some would say. I fell to the ground — "fainted" is how my family describes it. I remember feeling heavy and leaving my body, looking down at everyone but laughing inside. I then saw the panic on their faces. John and Amanda were not amused; they told me later that they and everyone else thought I was dead — I was so stiff, with hardly any pulse. Upon waking, with many blessings and holy water from the priest, I felt the greatest joy I had ever felt up to that time in my life. It was pure, sacred, holy, whole. I started to laugh. I laughed at the way we, as humans, think, act, talk and behave. I laughed at the way we take ourselves so seriously. I began to witness everyone, everything, in Technicolor. The world goes on, we leave at some point and we and everyone around us are saddened, but there is nothing to be sad about. It is truly all holographic. All is happening at once. Nothing is what is seems.

I laughed for days after this experience, and have been privileged to experience this time after time when I am in stillness, in meditation, both in Bali and in Almonte, Ontario, on the Trinity Table. Once you experience the power of this joy, this bliss, you are forever changed.

You can access this experience anytime. Some of us only need a few tools. After the suicide of our daughter Melanie, I went into a five-month period of turmoil. I was able to witness myself in grief, anger, denial and finally acceptance. But I have also had many days of joy and bliss. Allowing Spirit to have us is indeed empowering. There are days when Spirit guides you to allow the shadow to arise, to experience any grief you are in or the loss of something. Or you can experience the joy, the bliss of the Divine. You can find the laughter, the funny bone in you, any time you choose. Yes, it is that simple, and you do not have to go to Bali... though you can go if you want to.

Just for today...

... start dying to be awake; experiencing death is when we are fully awake.

DAY 226

The Spirit of I Am That

I Am That

What is this wild thing that has me in its grasp?
I feel as if I have been drunk for eight years
Drinking from the bowls, the rice of the gods.
Will I free myself, at last, at last?

It is with free will that I rested in the dream
If I wake how long will it take
To realize that in the dreaming
I awakened to a divinity that cannot be spoken,
only broken if I do not live its will?

The blade of grass, the women bent over in the rice fields,
I am that
The smell of rot, the song of gecko, the squeak of
pig ready for slaughter,
I am that
The fragrance of incense at temple, the scent of frangipani,
I am that

The rooster singing upon waking, the sun setting
over the swaying palms,
I am that
The labour, the stillness, the devotion of the workers,
I am that
The dancer, the gamelan, the laughter, the song,
This cannot be wrong
I am that.

This wild thing,
This energy that grips me
I take hold,
I will my will to not let go
The gods understand,
Here, I am every woman, every man
In balance
I am that

Just for today...

... let Spirit have you.

DAY 227

The Spirit of a Delete Button

I delete half of my day because of my thoughts.

In traffic, I have a negative thought when someone tailgates;

While shopping at a store, when someone is rude.

Whenever I have a shadow thought, I go into "delete, delete."

I am not my thoughts and I can stop them with a DELETE button.

In that present moment I can change that thought and think, "Just for today, only love." Watch your thoughts today. If they are negative, press your delete button.

Just for today...

... let the Spirit of Your Thoughts be only love.

Let Spirit have you. Only You can press Delete.

DAY 228

The Spirit of a Dark Night

Dark Night

I watch but do not see
I hear but do not answer
I feel but do not respond
These are choices, I do make
For your darkness
I am not willing to take
You are a magnificent mirror
For me to see
That you are the balance
For the light that is me.

Just for today...

... let the Balance of Light and Shadow have you.

DAY 229

August

Blue skies, the beauty of the trees full and alive,
The heat of an August day beckons.
Relax, read a good book, the sun on your face, perfection.
Surrender, it's summer, find a trail and start trekking.

Just for today...

... let the Spirit of Summer have you.

DAY 230

The Spirit of Awareness

My eyes are open to a silent illness. It kills the person, the family, the community. It is cunning, baffling, a thief. It disguises itself as a drug addict, alcoholic, shopping addict, power addict or gossip, to name a few.

We continue to live in the shadow of our four survival archetypes when we are not open to understanding the damage this illness causes.

Be aware, never afraid.

My brother Derek and our daughter Melanie took their own lives. How many times have you thought of it?

Mental illness is real. No one wants to talk about it.

It is time to talk. If not for ourselves, for future generations.

Light can only live in truth.

Just for today…

… let the Spirit of Awareness have you.

DAY 231

The Spirit of Faith

Emptiness is where I will rest on the waves of faith
Floating the crest of peace
Embracing the tides of compassion
With ripples of hope
As the jewels of sunlight sparkle through me
I am empty, except
I am filled with the love from thee.
Empty from the ever tormenting me.

Just for today...

... let the Spirit of Your Faith have you.

DAY 232

The Spirit of an Oprah Story

I received a call from Harpo Studios from a lovely woman by the name of M.

"Hello, is Lilly White available? This is M from Harpo Studios."

Who does not want to hear these words? I was at the store and M was calling me regarding the question I had emailed to them earlier that morning — a question I wanted Deepak Chopra to answer. They had asked if we were living our passion and whether we were working on any forgiveness issues. I was living my passion but not my highest potential. How did I know? I had been sick all the time since opening my store. Something was out of whack. I was taking what others said or wanted personally, and that was not how I expected to react.

The store had been opened just as Spirit had instructed me — to bring my love of Bali home instead of John and I retiring to Bali.

When M asked how this related to forgiveness, I replied that if we do not take people, places or things personally, there is nothing to forgive. Great. She gave me instructions about what to do when I was in Toronto at Oprah's conference.

I am on my way, excited. Imagine, I have a chance to be on Oprah — it's going to be amazing for business!

I arrive, meet a staff member, and am told that no, the question will not be asked/answered; I answered it already. Plus it is mostly related to business. Right church, wrong pew. The business of business.

Within the first hour, Bishop Jakes is telling us that we can be anything, do anything we give birth to. We are pregnant.

I almost faint in my chair. I am dizzy, confused, then bang, right to the heart, I hear Spirit: "Your business was a replacement for the fact that you have been estranged from your daughter for twenty years. You continue to give birth — to Power Up Your Life, Breakfast with Soul, the White Lilly, the Mayan Study group, Soul Journeys to Bali and more. God forbid if anyone should judge your achievements — they are attacking your motherhood."

I have been out there DOING instead of sitting still... instead of loving and knowing that when my daughter is ready (though it might take thirty years), she will come to me eventually. Or she may not. Yes, I have made my amends to her; she has not yet accepted them, but I do not need to substitute her by DOING and finding new ways to give birth.

I accept and surrender that she is unable to forgive me, but I have not yet surrendered to the pain of missing her and not seeing our three grandchildren.

How can spirit enter into this situation and heal it, heal our family, the old family dynamic that has been with us for generations? How can spirit heal if I am still substituting? I am not substituting with drinking or spending as I would have twenty-one years ago, but there is still that need to be first, to demand attention, to keep creating. Alas it is just that: substitution for being a bad mother.

There, I said it. Ya, I know, I did the best I could. But it was not the best for HER.

I will sit and feel the pain of missing her and our grandchildren. The pain of years lost. The pain of shame. I can "let Spirit have me."

Spirit loves me enough to let me know that no one could have given me the answer to my question — not Deepak, not Bishop Jakes, no one. I had the answer all the time. Like Dorothy when she found herself in Oz, there is chaos and confusion when we are called to search deeper, but there are always others to help along the way.

NOW I can love the store as it is — as a business, not as a child needing to be protected. Now I can heal. Now I can be in the store with the joy, wonder and spirit that it was created from.

I believe there is a sacred code to the universe — the I AM code, a loving code; when I am not in alignment with this code, I am NOT.

If you gave me the choice to be on Oprah today and receive all that goes with it, or to have this insight, I value the insight more. It is the insight I will take to Spirit when I draw my last breath.

With deep gratitude to Oprah, and a special thank you to M for that phone call.

Just for today...

... allow Your Spiritual Lessons to have you; they come from the least expected places!

DAY 233

The Spirit of Our Judge Archetype

To judge another without compassion, to judge with your anger, to judge another without knowing all the details of that person's circumstances, is a reflection of your own insecurities, your ego, your life.

Judging to such an extent as to speak in anger about someone is possibly why our bodies are sick.

Just for today...

... hold up a mirror,

let Spirit have YOU.

DAY 234

The Spirit of Our Saboteur

Another day in Paradise,

My daily salutation to the sunrise,

Out of nowhere a voice does ring,

To see the beauty in everything,

But what is this my feet do stamp?

The Saboteur sings, YOU NEED BOOT CAMP.

To those of you familiar with the Saboteur, when the shadow has its say,

It is our choice to embrace her, not keep her away.

Does not matter where I travel, it is my energy to unravel.

Just for today…

… let the Spirit of the Light Side of Your Saboteur have you.

DAY 235

Are You the One?

Are you the one to make a difference, when others are weeping, their homes, their lives are leaking. Do you think you are different?

Are you the one to live a congruent life, when there are those around you who feel they must give up their fight?

Are you the one to hold the space? When chaos reigns, can you be in grace?

Are you the one? When Spirit calls, will you accept the challenge, or will you run????

And if you run, will it be to thyself, where it has all begun?

Just for today...

... let the Spirit of Being the One to Make a Difference have you.

DAY 236

The Spirit of the Mask Being Removed

Your shadow has no place to hide. You are fully alive.
The you — the whole you — the holy you — wakes up from its slumber.
Your mask is removed, the eternal Om, this electrical charge, this current of life.

Flow embraces you fully in love.
Into the trance, this dance, you come alive, there is no more hiding.

YOU ARE ALIVE, in Harmony and Serenity.
Today, as you remove your mask, be aware, never afraid. Be YOU!

Just for today...

... let the Spirit of YOU, with no false self, have you.

DAY 237

The Spirit of Space

How many of us need space?

When you are in a group, notice how you do not want to get too close to others. That's okay — you need your space.

How do you feel when you are in a line — waiting, frustrated. That's okay, you just need your space. You feel blocked. It's not the best feeling, I agree.

I have been married forty years and I still need my space. I love sleeping alone. Yes, I like to cuddle, but after that, leave me in my sacred space. I can stretch, yawn, daydream, read, or listen to music without any distractions.

Call me selfish, but when I have my alone time I am much more expansive with others.

Just for today…

… find your Space, enjoy your Space.

DAY 238

The Spirit of a House Burning Down

Said the goddess to the fairy, "During this time it is important for you and John to remember three things on this journey, now that you have no home for your house has burnt down:

1. Be kind to one another.

2. Do not take anything or each other too seriously.

3. Remember to breathe and to let Spirit have you.

You have your weight scales, your magic mirror, your blender for protein shakes, and your coffee percolator — what more do you need?

In chaos, listen when Spirit speaks.

Just for today…

… let the Spirit of Chaos have you.

DAY 239

Let's Play, Pray

Let's play: I AM (fill in the blank about YOU)

__________________________ !

Let's pray: Thank you, Spirit, for this gift of

____________________________ !

Just for today…

… let the Spirit of Playfulness have you

I am playful, yippee!!

DAY 240

The Spirit of Self-Love

Your body is holy (whole), just as your soul.
Treat yourself with respect, as you would anything you feel has value.
Stop looking for others to validate you.
Heal yourself, heal the planet.

Just for today…

… let the Spirit of Self-Love have you.

DAY 241

The Spirit of Yoga

Yoga is not just for your body; it stretches you beyond your fearful boundaries.

Breathe, stretch, relax.

Just for today…

… let the Spirit of Stretching beyond Your Fears have you.

DAY 242

The Spirit of Angels

When we allow ourselves the gift of releasing judgment, anger, envy and pain, we allow the angels to enter and give us the experience of miracles.

Just for today…

… let the Spirit of Angels have you.

DAY 243

The Spirit of Financial Debt

Are you experiencing financial and emotional debt?

Wondering what decisions you made in the past allowed this chaos; what archetypes you are living out and have a desire to change?

Did you steal from your future unintentionally?

Did you believe that a money tree would grow out of the ethers?

You cannot have energetic debt without financial debt. They are one and the same.

Draw in your energy where it may be leaking. Let go of your worries, your desire to please, your anger, your jealously, your wounds. Eventually you will see your bank account fill up as you empty your life of negativity.

Forgive, move on, get creative, start paying back those debts in some small way. Call your bank. Tell them your situation. Ask for help. Let go of feeling humiliated. In time you will feel worthy again.

Just for today…

… let the Spirit of Getting out of Debt have you.

DAY 244

The Spirit of Your Archetypes

My granddaughter described me as part fairy, gypsy, hippie and madwoman.

She is very intuitive and wise.

What are your archetypes — those energies that help you reach your highest potential in this lifetime. Caroline Myss, *Sacred Contracts* and her newest book, *Archetypes*, will help you get started.

Ask a family member; they will know.

Fear not these energies, for they are your gatekeepers. They help you access your destiny.

Just for today…

…let the Spirit of Your Archetypes come through.

DAY 245

The Spirit of You

If you are still looking for someone to change your life...

Why are you not looking into the mirror?

Just for today...

... LOOK deep into YOU.

DAY 246

The Spirit of God's Will versus Free Will

What is God's will for us?

God's will, will always be in loving thoughts.

Remember, we have free will. That is God's pure love for us.

Whatever we do or say that is in light and has the intention of love is in alignment with Divine's will. Free will is not about control, although we may interpret it as such. Whenever you have a strong desire to say or do something, pay attention. Where is this coming from — your head or your heart? Where does it hit you in your body — your solar plexus? Listen to your stomach, and if your brain is in your stomach, it might be giving you an answer — perhaps not to your liking, but you have free will. What choose you? Love or fear?

Just for today…

…let the Spirit of Free Will have you.

DAY 247

The Spirit of Your Inner Traveller

"Every journey has a secret destination of which the traveller is unaware."
— Martin Buber

Whether we are in meditation, our dreams, or physically on our way somewhere, travel furthers our Divine Mission. How far are you willing to travel?

If your budget or time is an issue, as it is for most of us, read, Google, iBook, listen to tapes. The idea is to travel as far as you can, when you can. It is an education into the unknown. This education allows you to travel and understand yourself more by relating to others; to come to an understanding that we are all the same; to see that we are similar but have our unique differences.

Travel. Reach for the stars. They will light your way, shining forever on the essence of you.

Just for today...

... let the Spirit of Travel have you.

DAY 248

The Spirit of Why

Why are we still looking for gurus when our guru lives inside?

Why are we still requesting answers from others about what we should eat to stay healthy, when we come from the land of fresh and abundance.

Why are we still seeking when we have the eternal teacher/ student inside us?

We do not need to claim we know it all, but we can own what we do know.

Just for today...

... let your Internal Guru have you.

DAY 249

The Spirit of NO Thing

Just for one hour today, do not think. Just BE.

Dance, sing, move, walk, be in the presence of the Divine.

Allow spirit to move through you.

Be you. Let Spirit sing you.

Just for today…

…let the Spirit of No Thing have you.

DAY 250

The Spirit of Non-Judgment

Do you find yourself judging others, then blaming it on your mother?

Have you ever thought that when you judge, it is about you and not the other?

Just for today…

…let the Spirit of Non-Judgment have you.

DAY 251

The Spirit of a Fairy

Down the path is Tink
Over to the right is Bell
Turn left and Iris
will direct you to skip over to the pond of fairy dust.
There you will find YOU
May you have fairy dust at your feet,
Laughter in your belly and
Joy in your heart.

Just for today…

… let the Spirit of Playfulness have you.

DAY 252

The Spirit of Free Will

You have the gift of free will. Not making a decision IS a decision. What you put your energies into WILL happen as you WILL it.

Just for today...

... let the Spirit of Free Will have you.

DAY 253

The Spirit of Our Beliefs

What DO I believe? I believe in the power of prayer, the power of love, the power of acceptance, the awe of the raw, the wow of now.

On May 30th, 2012, at the age of thirty-seven, our daughter took her own life. She was a brilliant soul who was unable to see her own brilliance. Four days after her death we found out that my seventy-seven-year-old mother had stage-four colon cancer. A little later, my dad of seventy-nine years had a stroke, and I was in the process of closing my business, the White Lilly (a shop selling an ecological women's clothing line called Goddess on the Go). With all this stress, I developed shingles, symbolic of an old childhood issue resurfacing while parents are in distress. Two of my siblings had shingles at the same time. We live at a distance from one another, so this is symbolically brilliant.

I am telling you this not from a victim stance, but to illustrate that we can still live our highest potential despite whatever stress we are experiencing. I am reminded of Job in the Bible when he loses his child, his wealth, his health. It is only through his belief in God that he is able to accept what he cannot change. Living our highest potential is about acceptance, loving unconditionally, and understanding that no matter what is happening in or around us, it is all in divine order. Ours is not to reason why. I am to wake up each day with the question "How do I best serve?" not "Why do I deserve this?"

Prayer is a wonderful antidote to stress. Prayers sing to our hearts what we cannot perceive or hear with our minds.

There are many steps we can take; one of these steps is to not take ourselves so seriously. When we take our last breath, it will be between us and the God of our understanding. That last breath will allow us to leave with grace, and those who have gone on before us will give birth to our transition.

Just for today…

…let the Spirit of Your Beliefs have you.

DAY 254

The Spirit of Why Are You Here

Why did you come to Earth?

See yourself in a huge context. What is being born in you?

Get in touch with sacred impulse.

Your sacred purpose — what you want to give (not what you want to get) — not just you alone, but your soul's code; when you feel this, what do you need to do to realize it?

What are you most attracted to? To what area of life, of giving? Follow that attraction.

Find a group — what do you have in common? Become a sacred activist. What makes you angry? Whatever makes you angry, go change it. That just might be your soul calling.

Just for today...

... let the Spirit of Why You Are Here have you.

DAY 255

The Spirit of a God Box

Our grandson once asked, "Fairy Lilly, what is in this God box on your altar?"

I told him and asked, "What is in your God box?"

His answer: "My heart and my soul." The joy of children and the lessons they teach us.

Do you have a God box? A box you tell your secrets to, your heart's desire, your troubles, your truths? Start a God box today. Fill it up, empty it often. It symbolizes your ongoing progress.

Just for today...

... let the Spirit of Your God Box enlighten and lighten your burdens.

DAY 256

The Spirit of Releasing

Take this torn heart, I don't want it
Take this worn ego, I don't care for it
Take this old body, I don't feel it
Take this stale breath, I don't like its taste
Take this empty soul, I don't sense it
Take this suffering, I don't like repeating a pattern
Take this grief, I don't like weeping

Just for today...

... let the Spirit of Letting God Take What You Do Not Need have you.

DAY 257

The Spirit of Empowerment

You have unlimited power. You are a powerful empowered being. This power is how you create miracles. You live in balance of light and shadow. You create miracles through the light of your thoughts, feelings and actions.

Just for today...

... let the Spirit of Empowerment have you.

DAY 258

The Spirit of a Good Cup of Tea

Here is a recipe I developed with the help of my friend Suzanne Winlove-Smith. It includes seven ingredients and they are in alignment with your seven chakras. I call it Chakralicious. Enjoy.

Vanilla – 7th chakra – Christ consciousness
Star anise – 6th chakra – Eye opener; helps remove brain fog
Cardamom – 5th chakra – Speak truth clearly
Cinnamon sticks – 4th chakra – Warming heart
Ginger – 3rd chakra – Inner fire
Cloves – 2nd chakra – Relax muscles
Black pepper – 1st chakra – Grounding

Simmer on stove for an hour. Mix with hot milk, almond milk, coconut milk, or simply enjoy as is.

Just for today...

... let the Spirit of Chakralicious have you.

DAY 259

The Spirit of a Pioneering Soul

We are the universe, in person.

We are now awakening to who we are becoming.

It is our ego that invites spirit, the realm of our essence. Let us not beat up on ego.

We are the tree of life, growing daily, rooting, blossoming.

If you are empathic, you are picking up what is happening from the Earth and from others. How do you handle this energy? You let go; let God. Stop trying to control the outcome. How do you hold the Earth in your heart? You find your joy.

The timing for growing is a rapid pace, brisk and sudden; we know things immediately. And if we do not, we Google them.

You are a pioneering soul — go explore! What will you find out about yourself or others today?

Just for today…

…let Your Pioneering Soul have you.

DAY 260

The Spirit of the Veil

I have been hearing talk lately about "the veil." "The veil is coming down" or "The veil is thinning" or "The veil has lifted."

We are all trying our best to be more in alignment with the universe, spirit and those who have passed on to the other side. We have this capability; we were born with it... we are all from the same source, just different realms.

Our eyes are opening to something deeper, more real.

Let me play the devil's advocate and suggest that perhaps the veil is seeing for the first time the true intent of others. Perhaps the veil is our living and staying within our own guidelines of what truth is. I have had the experience of visiting a place known for its spirituality. Everywhere I went were signs posted: NO SMOKING, NO PARKING, NO FOOD, NO PETS, NO MUSIC, NO CANDLES, NO INCENSE. Would it be different if they said, "Thank you for not smoking," "Thank you for leaving your pets at home," "Thank you for understanding why we cannot have lit candles," etc.? A place that promotes spirituality and teaches us how to be authentic, but that continues to speak "NO" says something to me — a place that charges you a premium because you reserved your rooms forty-eight hours in advance instead of seventy-three hours. This does not speak of Spirit; it speaks of "You snooze, you lose. Sorry, hand over your cash!" The heck with the facts or the reasons why. "The communion within our community does not start here; it is about the almighty dollar. But we will discuss it as Spirit."

Let us be aware of what the spirit in a community is about and what the spirit of the almighty dollar is about.

Let us be awakened goddesses, not fools.

Just for today...

... let the Spirit of Truth have you.

DAY 261

The Spirit of Useful/Useless

When we are feeling useless, it is because we need to USE LESS of our energy so God can direct us; we need to be still.

When we are feeling useful, it is because we need to USE our energy to the FULlest capacity as God directs us; move with grace.

Just for today...

... let the Spirit of Being Still and Moving with Grace have you.

DAY 262

The Spirit of Spending

We were spending our resources like there was no tomorrow
Now we pay with all of our sorrows.

It was fun while it lasted, the shopping sprees
The trips and the dancing, where did it lead?

There was nothing to worry about, we will all be fine
We were young in age, a long way from fifty-nine.

There was so much to do, children to raise
Money was flowing, a large amount we were paid.

Month after month, year after year
We kept on spending, without any fear.

The past is upon us, we are up to our necks
It is time to unravel this thing we call "debt."

So the process begins, it is time to come clean
We won't spend anything; now that seems so mean.

Is it all or nothing, will we ever grow up?
We will start saving, twenty dollars in this cup.

We are not spending our resources, we are saving for tomorrow.
What a relief, no more sorrow.

Just for today...

... pay attention to your spending habits.

DAY 263

The Spirit of the Fall Equinox

A time to see and feel what you have accomplished as an individual and as a collective mind. Review your spring equinox intentions. (Mine was forgiveness — I had no idea what was to unfold.)

Did you create your creations?

Did you learn anything since the spring?

The fall equinox is when we get honest about what we are doing. If you're still working on some of your intentions, be clear about what you've already accomplished. I am sure if you sit still long enough you will see and feel that you are enough.

You will find your creations complete as they weave themselves into the collective mind.

If something you intended to create just didn't happen, don't give up, move forward. Ask yourself how important it is to you.

This fall…

… let Spirit have you and the Spirit of Your Intentions.

DAY 264

I am falling back into myself.
A time to be still, listen to spirit's will.
Thoughts falling from my head
Into my heart where ego stops and spirit starts.
Fall into grace with nothing to face but the beauty of me.
I change as the leaves on the branches, ever beauty, bright,
Swaying, adapting, getting ready to hibernate, to go deeper
To be free, free. To be me.

The season it is changing,
The breeze a brief decoy,
The sun sultry shining, the light it cannot destroy
As fall is silence unfolding, let us fall into Joy.

Just for today...

... let the Spirit of Fall have you.

DAY 265

The Spirit of Living Out Loud

You do not ask for permission to die — why would you need permission to live? Stop looking to others to tell you how. Just LIVE!

Let Spirit have you, just for today.

LAUGH OUT LOUD! No one is watching.

Just for today...

... let the Spirit of LOL have you.

DAY 266

The Spirit of Hardship

Hardship can make us more mature.

It can also be a clear sign that you are devoting your energy to things that are hindering, rather than helping, your spiritual growth.

Pay attention. Is your life really that hard? And, if it is, what do you need to change? Where do you need to redistribute your energies?

Pray about it. You will receive your answer.

Just for today...

... let the Spirit of Your Hardships have you.

DAY 267

The Spirit of Your Gifts

Co-create with your uniqueness — not with wanting to be like someone else or sameness, but with your abundance of gifts. Make a list of them today, and share one of these gifts with someone.

Be YOU today…

… let Spirit have you.

DAY 268

The Spirit of Reverence

Do something for someone today with reverence, with respect. There is no need to speak of your good deed.

Do not judge others, for the person you judge is only a reflection of what is in you.

Treat all those who come in your path today with respect.

Just for today...

... let the Spirit of Reverence have you.

DAY 269

The Spirit of Enough

Know that today you are ENOUGH.

Know you are filled to the brim with creativity; breathe the spirit of originality.

In the eyes of the Divine you are adequate.
Accept yourself just as you are, in the likeness and image of all that is and will be.

Just for today...

... be Enough.

DAY 270

The Spirit of Awareness

Be conscious of your every thought today, be aware of your every move, listen to your inner voice, pray from deep within.

Witness how your voice sounds when you raise your voice, when you feel fear, when you feel joy.

How fast, how slow do you eat? How aware are you of what you are eating, where it came from? What are your thoughts as you are eating?

What are you thinking when someone is talking to you? Are you listening or are you thinking of what to say next?

What needs to be changed? Be aware, not afraid, of these changes.

Just for today…

… let the Spirit of Awareness have you.

DAY 271

The Spirit of Observation

Observe where you can make a difference in the world.

Watch the news, follow your muse.

Being conscious of what is going on in the world allows you to change the world if that is your desire.

If you are afraid that watching the news and reading the headlines will affect you in a negative way, then you have no personal boundaries. Take what you need and pay no attention to the rest. You cannot change what you do not know.

Observe with non-judgment, non-attachment.

What affects you and makes you angry is a good starting point to get up and find a way to change it.

Information is knowledge, and knowledge can empower us.

Just for today...

... let the Spirit of Observation have you.

DAY 272

The Spirit of Your Body

Your Body is holy, just as your Soul is. Treat yourself with respect to become whole. Stop waiting or looking for someone to validate you. Heal yourself, heal the planet.

The Body of our planet is a reflection of our collective bodies.

We are only as sick as our secrets. Let's get honest and clear out the old. Bring in the new — new ideas, new hopes, new decisions.

Just for today...

... be respectful of Your Body.

DAY 273

The Spirit of Burnout

Feeling burnt out allows us to touch the fire within.

Sometimes burnout is Spirit's way of telling us that we added too much fuel to our daily endeavors. Sometimes we move, speak, do, make decisions and judge much too quickly. Burnout is nature's way of saying, "Time out — go to your room."

Once in our room, we can tune in to our sacred space and move deeper into ourselves — not in a depressed way, but in a caring, loving, compassionate way. This is called maturity. Once we are rested our fire will return, but not filled with an all-consuming combustion that ignites and burns quickly once again, but with a desire to radiate the light that we are.

Just for today...

... learn the lessons of Burnout.

DAY 274

Realms

I work with the four realms that we are born into. There are many more, but in working with the archetypes I have discovered that these four represent the four survival archetypes, the four strains of DNA. Any other realms that Doreen Virtue writes about are actually archetypes. I have found that when we know ourselves through the realms, we can stop judging others. For example, a Fairy, better known as the Elemental, likes to flirt, and if she is in the presence of a Star, who is shy and withdrawn, the Star's shyness is not because the Star does not like her; they just do not vibrate at the same frequency. It is all very simple really.

Fairy, Star, Angel, Wise One... In the following days discover which realm you originate from.

Just for today...

... let the Spirit of YOUR Realm have you.

DAY 275

The Spirit of the Angel Realm

Those from the Angel realm — the lovers, those who are co-dependent — are service-oriented: nurses, counselors, librarians... anything to be of service. They often have weight issues, hold weight inside; they don't want to upset the status quo, so they keep things inside, thus the weight. They may have heart issues, cannot give and receive equally; the hands are attached to giving and receiving, and if not able to receive, the heart becomes imbalanced.

I often hear, "They were such an angel, how could they have died of a heart attack?"

They love detail and like to change people. You do not want to see an Angel in a relationship with a Fairy. The Angel wants to change them, so the relationship is a very co-dependent one. The Fairy stirs up trouble, the Angel rescues. The cycle continues until the Fairy becomes wise, rescues itself, and the Angel is then left alone, but not for long; they are on their way to save another. One day the Angel may realize, "I want to live and love in balance, look after myself for a change and learn to receive and give equally."

Angels usually have the Divine Child archetype. Or they may have the Abandoned Child, thus their need to rescue. They often also have the following archetypes: Mother, Servant, Slave, Goddess.

Health issue: Heart

Work on this planet: Service

Just for today...

... let the Spirit of Your Archetypes have you.

DAY 276

The Spirit of the Elemental Realm

The Elemental realm holds the fairies and elves. Characteristics of Elementals include having difficulty with being stuck indoors over a long period of time. They are restless, chatty, love attention, likely have an addiction of some sort and go outside themselves for their fulfillment. Very creative, they do not like to follow rules, have a great sense of humour, and are playful and mischievous. They often have the archetypes of Addict, Thief, Gambler, Puck, Magical Child. They can relate to the trees, talk to them, and plant flowers with a knowingness that someone else is looking after the plant. They are not even sure who or why — it is just a feeling, until they understand their realm...

Health issues: Stomach, low self-esteem, ulcers

Work on this planet: Communicators

Are you an Elemental?

Just for today...

... let the Spirit of Your Archetypes have you.

DAY 277

The Spirit of the Star Realm

I have only met two clients in the last four years who are from the Star realm and did not have the Orphan Child archetype.

These people are different. Some have Asperger's or another form of autism.

They are highly evolved in spirit.

They feel different when we are around them; we call them weird. They have guides from other planets. As children these Stars asked questions such as "What am I doing here?" "Who are these people in my family?" "I am sure I was adopted."

They are wallflowers and do not like to draw attention to themselves. Very sensitive, withdrawn looking, and prone to allergies, they are the reiki masters, healers, loving and sensitive — hands-on healing. I am convinced that most from Bali and Hawaii are Stars, hence great massagers.

They teach us about crystals and usually have archetypes such as Hermit, Engineer, Visionary, Mystic, Lover.

Health issues: Skin disorders, allergies.

Work on this planet: Healers. All they want to talk about is healing with love.

Just for today...

... let the Spirit of Your Archetypes have you.

DAY 278

The Spirit of the Wise One Realm

Ah, the Wise Ones. Growing up they know it all, and that is because somewhere in them, they do.

They are the co-creators with the universe, according to Doreen Virtue. Sometimes dark in nature, they have difficulty having fun, taking themselves too seriously. "Anal-retentive" is how I describe them, but they are brilliant. If you give a Wise One their wand, and if at that point they did not know who they were, look out; they will move the mountain. They know how, and it is done... They sometimes have a widow's peak. They are the wizards, sometimes drawn to astrology. I have also seen the Wise One as the Shaman, Witch, Alchemist, Teacher, Guide, Mentor, or Mystic.

They were beheaded and burned at the stake in past lives, and in this lifetime usually have throat issues and digestive problems. They hold on to their anger in their digestive tract (anal-retentive).

Work on this planet: Teachers

Just for today...

... let the Spirit of Your Archetypes have you.

DAY 279

The Spirit of the Call

I awaken from a deep slumber to a sound in the corner
of the room.
But wait, is that thunder?
Or the sound of my heart as I witness you staring back at me.
Oh God, you are here.
I am filled with passion as you whisper in my ear,
"I am not here to devour you, do not fear.
Because of your faith in me, you answered the call, your destiny.
I will take you to the spring of your childhood where your joy
has been but a journey to the heartland of your own creation.
Go back to sleep now and continue to live your dreams."

Just for today...

... let the Spirit of Your Dreams have you.

DAY 280

The Spirit of the Goddess

I am unravelling the old to stitch in the new

I am weaving thyself around the fabric of my inner self

I am threading the needle to blend shadow into thy light

I am placing this wrapping of love onto my beloved's shelf

When my beloved, this god/goddess who loves me with defects

Takes me down to breathe through me

And shows me how my willingness has a cause and effect

I will dance in joy as I have come to realize all this unravelling,
weaving, threading has made me whole

Casting this needle of light right through my soul

Just for today...

... let Spirit have you.

DAY 281

The Spirit of Bali

There is a simple breeze
It is here for you and me
On the shores of Bali

The sun is always glowing
As the boats are rowing
On the shores of Bali

As you watch the children dance
To the songs they chant
You're reminded of the flow
It's here, it's there, it's everywhere you go
On the shores of Bali

It's your song they sing
Your divinity within
On the shores of Bali

Don't let the clouds fool you
For the sun is shining through
On the shores of Bali

Right into your cells
You'll remember well
The moon, heaven and stars
Wake up, wake up to who you really are
On the shores of Bali

There is a wishing well, it's yours to fill
With the hopes of all your tomorrows
Put away your past, you are free at last
Today, no more sorrow
On the shores of Bali

There is a portal here
Perhaps everywhere
That speaks of grace
Not what we acquire or the look of our face
On the shores of Bali

It is the tiny decisions
You make each moment
To breathe in your peace
You are the breeze in motion
On the shores of Bali

Your heart is released
From the bondage of self
Compassion for others
Is where spirit does dwell
Here
On the shores of Bali

This portal, you cannot see
It's for you and me
On the shores of Bali

So take your time
Spirit will make up your mind
When to visit the shores of Bali

Remember this
You can live your bliss
On the shores of Bali...

Just for today...

... let the Spirit of Bali have you.

DAY 282

The Spirit of Rest

The Rest of Me

When my last breath of delight is in the universe
When my eyes close to enter the cosmos
Free me to the breeze of Bali, to the shores of home
For there you will find me.

Just for today…

… let the Spirit of Rest have you.

DAY 283

The Spirit of the Spell

The spell needs to be broken
Here is my token
As you prepare to take leave
"If you continue to live in your ancestral dream
Your world will be dark, bitter and unclean.
Wake up, wake up, for you have missed the mark:
Love, forgiveness, compassion,
Is the wand to your heart."

Just for today…

… let the Spirit of the Spell have you.

DAY 284

The Spirit of Your Nature

We are of nature.

We are very much like the weather — sunny, stormy, foggy, temperate, ever-changing. Hot, cold, weeping (rain). We may be able to forecast our moods; our radar goes up (boundaries) when a windy front moves in, and much like the trees, we bend and hold our ground.

It's all natural. We are of the earth; we will return to the earth.

Just for today...

... let the Spirit of Your Nature have you.

Be a force of nature and accept yourself.

Witness and adjust.

DAY 285

The Spirit of Thanksgiving

The turkey was purchased at Don's
The cranberries stewing
I will shape them into a swan
Pumpkin cake, Amanda will make
Whatever we eat is sure to be sweet
For Thanksgiving is here, abundance everywhere
Gratitude for family and friends
Allowing the Spirit of Thanksgiving,
The Spirit of our ancestors, to have me.

Celebrate today any way you are able. It does not have to be anything fancy or even with family. Do whatever feels right for you, but give thanks.

Just for today...

... let the Spirit of Thanksgiving have you.

DAY 286

The Spirit of Boundaries

For years I have lived, loved, taught and accepted healthy boundaries. After all, I was taught by one of the greatest mentors/teachers I know. You could not have lived in the family I was raised in without learning boundaries at some point. But healthy boundaries are interesting when we are not witnessing ourselves regularly or paying attention.

We need to know who we are, and who we are not. Can I set limits and still be loving? Ah, there lies the challenge for me. Sometimes yes, sometimes no, especially if I have just gotten off the phone with difficult news. My boundaries go out the door, and when I do set them they are with rudeness, only because my heart is hurting at that time. If I hurt someone because of my boundaries and my intent was to be loving, then they in time will come to understand. If my intent was to hurt, then I apologize.

Think about your boundaries, and believe in yourself enough to live them. Be healthy enough to have them.

Just for today…

… let the Spirit of Your Personal Boundaries have you.

DAY 287

The Spirit of "Ya, But"

Do you suffer from the ya-buts?

How many times a day are you challenged in some way, responding with "Ya, but I _________."

How many times a day do you feel like you have to defend yourself with a "Ya, but"? If you use "Ya, but," you are possibly making things up.

Just for today...

... witness yourself and your ya-buts; answer with yes / no. Ya-buts be gone.

DAY 288

The Spirit of Your Soul

Your soul always knows, guides you, never told

Wakes you in the morning with just a hint of a kiss

Prays with you at night with gratitude, not a moment in your day to be missed

Your soul will speak to you in your dreams, awakening what is inside, guiding you, soul will assist.

Just for today

... let the Spirit of the Truth of Your Soul have you.

DAY 289

The Spirit of Prayer

What if prayers change your life?

A few years ago a friend mentioned to me that she did not like saying some of our Catholic prayers, particularly the Act of Contrition. Telling or praying to a God she felt was going to judge her was not her gig. God felt to her like a domineering father figure she had to confess to.

While out on my walk one morning, I began to say the rosary. Usually when I am walking or exercising I use that time and opportunity to pray. I was thinking of the Act of Contrition and how when we change our perspective of the wording, it embraces us, it tells our story, it directs us. When I say, "Oh my God I am heartily sorry for offending thee," I am talking to Gaia, the living Earth, the collective. Have I been attentive, conscious of what is going on with our planet? I am talking to the kingdom that also lives inside me.

Spirit gave us free will. "Thy will be done, on Earth as it is in heaven." Think about those words. I walk on Earth, but heaven resides in and around, above and beyond me. When I say the Our Father, I am talking to the Universal Source that bonds us. When I repeat the Hail Mary, I am loving and affirming the divine goddess/feminine energy in each of us. I am blessing all that is, has been and will be.

So WHAT IF we change our perspective — not the words of the prayers but how we feel about them. It can be a religious prayer, a poem, a word, a devotion. Prayers have been with us for centuries. They must have some power. What if your life changes because of your PRAYERS?

Just for today…

… let the Power of Prayer have you.

DAY 290

Listen to Your Heart

Listen to your heart, it speaks to you

Speak to your heart, it loves you

When YOU love you

You will have more to share with others with an open heart

Just for today…

… let the Spirit of Your Heart have you.

DAY 291

The Spirit of Conscious Choices

Living your highest potential, will not drive you mental

It's about making conscious choices, when we hear negative voices

It's as simple as taking a breath, remove yourself from doubt, take a step

Now how does your body feel? The question you asked is real

Listen with your heart, that is what sets you apart, from a life that is heavy and dull to living your life with love

Just for today...

... let the Spirit of Your Conscious Choices have you.

DAY 292

The Spirit of Dressing for the Divine

The sun, the food, the spices, the smells, the heat, the ocean, the frangipani.

Heaven on Earth — I am alone in Bali and getting ready to go to dinner.

At night I dressed for the Divine... for the love of the Divine... a thank you for my existence.

As you are dressing today, remember the people who made the fabric, and who sold the clothes to you. Remember you are dressing carefully, not just for yourself but for the Divine. Give thanks that you are indeed blessed.

Just for today...

... let the Spirit of Dressing for the Divine have you.

DAY 293

The Spirit of Clothes

As you dress yourself today, know that
It is NOT the clothes that give you confidence,
It's your confidence that makes the clothes.

Just for today...

... wear your Confidence with Style.

DAY 294

The Spirit of Freedom

Why try to fit in when you can stand up, stand out, shout out:

I am free, I am ME!

Just for today…

… let the Spirit of Self-Confidence have you.

DAY 295

The Spirit of Your Saboteur

I went to the doctor and the doctor said,
"Girl, you are silly, now shake your head.
Get your body moving, for Goddess's sake,
Never mind eating the cake that you just baked.
Get up in the morning and strengthen those thighs,
Dance every evening, extra pounds wave, bye, bye, bye!"

Just for today…

… do not let the Spirit of Your Saboteur have you; get moving!

DAY 296

The Spirit of Bravery

Are you brave enough to look — really look — at all the things you never wanted to see?

Sometimes you might have to look back to see ahead.

Just for today...

... let the Spirit of Your Brave Self have you.

DAY 297

The Spirit of Saint Valentine

I still love my ex-boyfriend; he became my knight forty years ago.

"There is a story about Saint Valentine's key. It is a charm used in the province of Padua, Italy. It is a metal key named after Saint Valentine, the patron saint not only of love and marriage but also of epilepsy, traditionally known as Saint Valentine's Malady. The key is gifted as a romantic symbol and an invitation to 'unlock the giver's heart.'"
—Wikipedia

What is in your heart that you would like to unlock? Does someone else hold the key? Are you afraid to love? Does it disempower you? Do you love too much? Do you love someone who cannot love you back?

Take your inner key today and unlock the answers to any questions you might have about love — either finding love or loving yourself.

If you are happy and in a relationship, celebrate with gratitude.

Just for today...

...let the Spirit of Love have you.

DAY 298

The Spirit of Courage

Do you remember the song "The Gambler" by Kenny Rogers, which had the words "You gotta know when to fold them"? It takes courage to take a risk and more courage to know when to walk away.

"Courage: the choice and willingness to confront agony, pain, danger, uncertainty or intimidation. Physical courage is courage in the face of physical pain, hardship, death or threat of death, while moral courage is the ability to act rightly in the face of popular opposition, shame, scandal or discouragement."

—Wikipedia

We need courage daily. It took courage when I opened my store in 2011, and more courage to close it in 2014 (because of tragic events in our family during those years).

It takes courage to start a new job and courage to know when to quit. Courage to say yes, and courage to say no.

We need an abundance of courage to stand up for our rights, to fight for others, and to know when to walk away. These are just a few examples of courage. You may have many more of your own.

Just for today…

… let the Spirit of Courage lead you through your day.

DAY 299

The Spirit of Time

Time waits for no one,

No one should wait for time.

Just for today…

… let Timelessness have you.

DAY 300

The Spirit of Bliss

Death is Deadly

Life is Lively

Happiness is Healthy

BUT,

Bliss is Believing anything is possible.

Just for today...

... let the Spirit of Bliss have you.

DAY 301

The Spirit of Peace

Let there be peace in you today. Believe that there can be peace everywhere you look today.

First find that peaceful spot inside you; someone or something will try to steal that peace. Pretend you are a pirate today and safeguard your own jewels, one of them being peace.

Just for today...

... let the Spirit of Peace have you.

DAY 302

The Spirit of Challenge

You can climb every mountain on this planet, but only when you reach into your heart, rise above your ego and feel compassion and forgiveness will you reach your peak, your highest potential.

Just for today…

… let the Spirit of Forgiveness have you.

DAY 303

The Spirit of Love

I love all things real
I love the pain, the tears that feel like rain,
as they float down the cheeks
this is life, I feel

I love all people who are real
their smiles, their struggles
their need to snuggle
their beliefs, their grief
their desire to Be
their willingness to see.

I love all animals who are wanting
they eat, they sleep
they love, sometimes taunting

I love the sun, the moon, the planets
their brightness, the stars
forever foretelling our fate, if today it is all about Mars.

I love what is real,
this journey, this never-ending wheel
of what IS, the real deal
Life, no fight
just being, seeing, believing.

Just for today...

... let the Spirit of Love have you.

DAY 304

The Spirit of Your Dreams

What are your dreams?

What do your nightly dreams tell you?
What about your daydreams?

Our dreams are our subconscious getting our attention. They are telling us something we may have forgotten or hidden. The energy taking shape is not really a dream; it is our desires, our wishes, our creativity taking shape.

Dream big! Dream your own existence into a divine reality.

Just for today…

…let the Spirit of Your Dreams have you.

DAY 305

The Spirit of Humour

When life gets tough, as it sometimes will,
And the road you take seems all uphill,
Remember what the angels tell us when we are still:
"Your weapon is HUMOUR and not a pill."

Just for today...

... let the Spirit of Humour have you.

DAY 306

The Spirit of Love versus Fear

Love everything, everyone

Fear nothing, no one

Love will always affect you in ways that lift you up

Fear will always affect you in ways that bring you down

Just for today…

… let the Spirit of Love have you.

DAY 307

The Spirit of Your Journey

On your journey, prayer is your fuel and love is your fill-up.

Just for today…

… let the Love of Your Journey fill you up.

DAY 308

The Spirit of Battles

There are battles and wars everywhere. The first one we need to heal is the battle within ourselves.

You are a Divine Being of Light. Shine through the tough times of your battles. Be a warrior for your soul.

There is no need to defend yourself, God knows. Do not depend on others; if they are unavailable, God is.

Just for today…

… let the Spirit of Your Battles have you;

they will make you stronger.

DAY 309

The Spirit of Colour

Have you ever noticed that there are colours that attract you and colours that repel you? Pay attention — which one is your favourite right now?

Which chakra are you presently working on? Is your favourite colour yellow and you are working on your self-esteem? Is it bright cobalt blue and you are learning to speak your truth?

If you are still unaware of chakras — what I like to call the organs of the soul, read more about them. You will find everything you need on Google.

As the prism of colour is reflected into your eyes, it reaches your heart; you are ready to CHANGE.

Just for today...

... let the Spirit of Colour have you.

DAY 310

The Spirit of Listening

Do we listen to be heard
or do we listen to be ahead of the herd?
Do we look into their eyes
or do we wear our mask, our daily disguise?
Listening to connect with our hearts
to allow the other to know, we are in tune
Listening to their song,
to their creativity, their art, that they belong.

Just for today…

… let the Spirit of Listening have you.

DAY 311

The Spirit of YES

How many times a day do you say YES... or do you say NO first without thinking?

Do you feel YES and say NO?

Is your brain on auto pilot?

Imagine saying YES — allow the process.

If at first you say NO, the negative is more difficult to remove.

Just for today...

... let the Spirit of Your YES have you.

DAY 312

The Spirit of the World of In-Between

Have you ever had a dream
In the world of in-between?
My brother Derek, who had passed so long ago,
Just popped in to say hello.
I remember his energy, his smell, his face.
We had a chat in our sacred space.
When it was time to say goodbye,
No need for tears or to badly feel,
For upon awakening I realize,
The world of in-between is what is real.

Just for today…

… let the Spirit of Those Who Have Passed say "Hello."

DAY 313

The Spirit of Winter

The winter of my heart is so cold
I witness the dying of the young and the old
I feel like I am losing everything, everyone.

I remember the summer, the heat of love
The spring of new beginnings in any relationship
The letting go, the starting over
The dreams of all to come
And I realize that in the fall
It's time to go inward so I can feel and fuel my inner fire
So the winter will not freeze my heart forever
That I will chill out and not see everything as barren.

Just for today…

… let the Spirit of Winter have you.

DAY 314

The Spirit of Prayer

I'm praying today for Gaza
and what do you think I hear?
Yes, Lilly, pray for all who are suffering,
the children, their families so near.

For you see the world is now smaller
your prayers are heard even now
a prayer vigil is needed
by everyone, yes on your knees and bow

So we will pray each day for Gaza
that a continued truce will prevail
and in the land once known as Canaan
we will know peace without fail

Let us all continue to pray
and let us all pray on a certain day
call it a Prayer Vigil for Gaza
and help end this dreadful human saga.

Just for today...

...let the Spirit of Prayer have you.

DAY 315

The Spirit of Enough

Into the depths of my being
I awoke seeing
The possibilities laid before us this beautiful day.

Suddenly I was filled with fear
At someone else's despair

Her belief that she is not enough
Her confusion of being
Has limited love's space to dwell where it's not safe
The shame of truly showing one's face
To stand up and say I am filled with grace
Into this community I rise up and take my place

A place filled with wonder, joy and play
Living today there is a new way
Of shining her light
She is part of one community
Her duty

To be conscious of those around
To look with gratitude, joy, sharing, passion
She is a Beacon of Light, bright in Unity

Just for today…

… let the Spirit of Being Enough have you.

DAY 316

The Spirit of Gratitude

Gratitude comes in many forms.

Grateful for the peace we feel when we are in the midst of chaos.
Grateful for the belief in someone when they emotionally abandon us.
Grateful for hope when all seems lost.
Grateful for wisdom when we need to let go.
Grateful for serenity when we are deep in grief.

Yes, gratitude is expressed in many ways. Grace of gratitude does not have to be a person, place or thing.

Just for today...

... let the Spirit of Gratitude have you.

DAY 317

The Spirit of Thanksgiving

As I write, it is Thanksgiving weekend here in Canada. I am in the vibration of GRATITUDE — the attitude of a remarkably powerful force, a force that once unleashed can start a project, heal a body, commune with a community, create a miracle and give hope to a planet.

Giving without any hidden agenda. The pleasure of sharing. Receiving in joy. A simple thank you.

When we are mindful, it is so much easier to be in gratitude.

Look around; take a breath. Air, thank you. Sky, thank you. The leaf falling with its fire-red hue, thank you.

The more thankful you become for all the abundance around you, the love that is in you, the more abundance will flow through you. Take another deep breath, the breath of life, look up, there you will see, feel Spirit. Be thankful. You never know what the clouds, the sky, the universe have to give back to you.

Be open to receive.

Just for today…

… let the Spirit of Thanksgiving have you.

DAY 318

The Spirit of Acceptance

Disappointment is the Universal Source telling you that new plans are on the horizon.

You are not conscious of them yet.

Accept all is in divine order.

Just for today...

... let the Spirit of Acceptance have you.

DAY 319

The Spirit of Change

When we identify and change what we need to change within ourselves, we don't have time to judge others.

Just for today…

… let the Spirit of Change have you.

DAY 320

The Spirit of Perspective

GOD, Help Me.

HELP Me, God.

All in perspective.

Just for today…

… let the Spirit of Your Perspective have you.

DAY 321

The Spirit of Pain

When in pain, TALK it out — do not SHOUT it out.

Just for today...

... let the Spirit of Understanding have you.

DAY 322

The Spirit of Light

Our darkest hour is usually our finest moment.

Relax into whatever is happening.

Breathe into the light of whatever is happening.

Just for today...

... let the Spirit of Light have you.

DAY 323

The Spirit of 4H Club

When we have HEALTH, we have HOPE
When we have HOPE, we are HAPPY
When we are HAPPY, we are in HEAVEN

Just for today…

let the Spirit of 4H have you.

DAY 324

The Spirit of Youth

You were young once, remember?

Youth is eternal... NOW, go play!

Just for today...

... let the Spirit of Play have you.

DAY 325

The Spirit of Self-Esteem

When you develop self-esteem
Kindness flows
Your words do not criticize or judge
Your words inspire others
To be their best

Just for today...

... let the Spirit of Kindness have you.

DAY 326

The Spirit of Light

You are light energy

You have the power

You have the power to change that which is dark into light

This is your spiritual quest

You have the tools available to you

Just for today…

… let your Spiritual Quest lead you.

DAY 327

The Spirit of the Divine

When we die we go back into the collective. There are no pearly gates and we will not see Santa Claus. We will be greeted by energy, the collective of spirits, perhaps a family member, a love one, a noble friend.

We will not be judged, either in light or shadow. There are only observations. We come into this lifetime with free will and a sacred contract, so the collective does not want anything or require anything from us.

Suffering is part of the human experience, and what allows one person to suffer may not affect the other. Again, it depends on our sacred contract. Our loved ones observe and it is up to us to ask for their assistance. This assistance is not tangible; it comes in the form of peace, hope, love, joy, forgiveness. That is all we ever really need — that and acceptance. With these tools we can move mountains, help where needed, serve the universe with grace and prayer.

Just for today...

... allow what is to be.

DAY 328

The Spirit of Meditation

Give yourself a break this season by taking eleven minutes each day, from December 1st through December 31st, to meditate in the morning, noon or evening.

Take a breath, be still, let Spirit have you.

Many people talk about being the change. You run around trying to make change, which sometimes can be confusing.

It can be as simple as putting your feet up, focusing on the spirit within you, and embracing the spirit of your ancestors, the spirit of oneness, the spirit of Jesus, Buddha, Krishna, or anyone else who resonates with your soul. "Let go; let God." Beginning today, take a break for your soul.

Who knows, by the new year you will have started a new ritual for your self, your soul.

Remember to create a small altar, a gift to you this season. It will alter your consciousness.

Season's greetings and the merriest Christmas ever.

Just for today...

... let the Spirit of Meditation have you.

DAY 329

The Spirit of Change

We are told that a single soul who turns from the negative to the positive and starts to do acts of loving kindness can alter the world.

It is also written that if you save one soul, it is as if you've saved the entire world.

Are you that person?

Just for today...

... let the Spirit of Change have you.

DAY 330

The Spirit of Your Destiny

Some people say that you cannot control what happens to you; you can only control your reaction to it. However, what you have learnt thus far is that everything is circular. That means that your reaction to an event today is actually a seed for an event/effect tomorrow.

In truth, you DO control your destiny... with your reactions.

Just for today...

... let the seeds of your thoughts in the light bring you to Your Destiny.

DAY 331

The Spirit of Dirty Dishes

There's nothing like sitting down to a meal. Unfortunately there's nothing more annoying than standing over the sink afterward cleaning the dishes. Usually I say, "Tomorrow... I will clean them tomorrow." Dear God, the mess in the morning is so annoying.

As annoying as dirty dishes can be, they are a burden if I do not handle them right away.

This is life.

My soul is like a dish. It starts out clean, but every time I act without consciousness I dirty it. If I do not clean up my mess right away, it lingers and sticks to my soul. The longer I leave the dirt, the more pain there is involved in cleaning it.

Face your dirty dishes today. Remember all the instances when you didn't clean up your mess. Remove all the layers that are haunting you. Start today with a clean slate.

Just for today...

... let the Spirit of Cleaning Up have you.

DAY 332

The Spirit of Our Walls

It is possible to be right next to a person, yet still be far away.

Where are you? Where are your thoughts?

People build walls around themselves with thoughts. We don't let others in because we are not present.

Notice when your thoughts take you out of the moment today. Find a way to tear down your walls. Be excited about everyone you are connected to this day.

Just for today...

... let the Spirit of Tearing Down Your Walls have you.

DAY 333

The Spirit of Gossip

Evil speaking, or gossiping, is one of the worst things you can do. It brings negativity to the person who is gossiping, to the person who is being gossiped about, and to the person who is listening to the gossip.

Every time we say something negative, we create a negative vibration.

Shudder when you hear gossip. Walk away, do not exchange. Live and let live.

Just for today...

... let the Spirit of Right Speaking have you.

DAY 334

The Spirit of God

We do not become closer to God by meditating on a mountain and shutting out all our desires. We become closer by loving, even those we do not like.

We are really here to find new ways to deal with one another.

What choose you this day — love or the desire to be right?

Choose God; that is love. If you do not believe in God, use Good Orderly Direction.

Just for today...

... let the Spirit of GOD have you.

DAY 335

The Spirit of Success

When we climb the ladder to success, eventually we may cause chaos somewhere. It could be with our kids, our spouse, our health, our finances.

In other words, many people spend their entire lives living in a reactive mode because it appears to have worked for them, and in the twilight of their lives, when it is almost too late to change, they lose all their success.

I hope this isn't too scary. It's meant to be a wake-up call. Check in with yourself today. Are you on a reactive road to success? If so, it's not too late to change!

What does success mean to you? A good job, a healthy body, a loving family?

In later years it is not too late to change; we understand what true success is. It might be playing with our grandchildren, having good friends, understanding that death is an ongoing process of our evolution. It might be a simple understanding that we are love. Now that is success.

Just for today...

... let the Spirit of Success have you.

DAY 336

The Spirit of Our Words

What — did you really think that our words
do not cast spells?

There are many negative forces that attempt to block and impede us. We create these negative forces with our own harmful words and actions. Our words travel through the spiritual network. We bring them into our being.

The first step to right speaking to is to bless everything we say. Let us stop cursing that driver, complaining to a shopkeeper or judging one another;
let's say something positive.

Cast a new spell.

Just for today...

... let the Spirit of Your Words have you.

DAY 337

The Spirit of Rewards

Have you noticed that everywhere we look there are rewards? Air rewards, shopping rewards...

It's easy to get caught up in wanting the end result instead of embracing the process.

The strength we develop during the process of the activity is our true reward.

Just for today...

... let the Spirit of Strength have you.

DAY 338

The Spirit of Wealth

Henry David Thoreau said, "Wealth is the ability to fully experience life."

Where is your wealth? Is it in your office, the car you drive, your home, your clothes, your jewels? You can become a slave to your wealth if you do not understand that the richness of your wealth is your family, your children, your friends, your community.

If you are blessed to be wealthy and have financial success, enjoy your abundance; never apologize for the benefits of your labour. Share where you are able, embrace your wealth, family, friends and community.

Just for today…

… let the Spirit of Your True Wealth have you.

DAY 339

The Spirit of Enough

You come into this world in nakedness and you will leave in nakedness.

What is in between is for show and tell.

What will you leave behind? Have you loved enough? Did you give enough?

Did you allow enough joy, peace and happiness to enter your heart?

What will you give away when you leave?

Just for today...

... let the Spirit of Doing Enough and Being Enough have you.

DAY 340

The Spirit of Challenges

Challenges come to teach us something,
to make us stronger.

Do you have the soul stamina to face everyday challenges?

Once we understand what the real purpose of today's challenge is, we will see the truth. Challenges are opportunities for personal growth.

Just for today...

... let the Spirit of Today's Challenge have you.

DAY 341

The Spirit of Relationships

In most relationships people do not need to make as many demands on each other as they do. If they have mutual security, they are free to be who they are.

To be in a relationship and still be free is one of the greatest gifts you can give each other; no obsessing, jealousy, control. No demanding attention. We feel free, are loved deeply; we love and maintain our relationship. We love the other as we love ourselves.

Just for today...

... let the Spirit of Relationships have you.

DAY 342

The Spirit of Complete

As you go about your day, your labours and your responsibilities today, remember you do not have to be perfect, you only need to be complete.

When you encounter something about yourself that you don't like, resist the temptation to beat yourself up.

You are not here to judge yourself; you are here to keep going. Embracing this consciousness changes your life. This consciousness makes you complete.

Just for today...

... know you are Complete.

DAY 343

The Spirit of Risks

Taking a risk is a great way to get out from under the slavery of fear.

Risk is uncomfortable... but it is brave. And if it's done for the sake of creating something for someone or for the world — bravo.

Taking a risk means things can go wrong and we might be criticized or attacked.

Taking a risk means putting our ego on the line. It means rolling with our heart and not our head.

Just for today...

... let the Spirit of Risk-Taking have you;

Fear not. Go for it!

DAY 344

The Spirit of Your Voice

We express ourselves in many ways — through our style, our home, the car we drive, our voice.

How do you express yourself? Do you have a worried tone; a happy, joy-filled tone; a defiant tone?

Your voice is the next thing others notice after they notice your looks. Is it high-pitched, low-pitched, gruff, pleasant?

Pay attention today to how you carry your voice. Speak clearly and openly. Speak with freedom in your heart and others will be attracted to the voice of the angels.

Just for today...

... let the Spirit of Speaking Clearly have you.

DAY 345

The Spirit of Blessings

It's beginning to look a lot like blessings,
Everywhere I go,
A smile on the street,
With everyone we meet
The heart it does expand,
A child, woman or man
The spirit of serving is here,
A perfect time of year
To remember all our gifts,
With gratitude our lives will shift
Yes, it's beginning to look a lot like blessings.

Just for today…

… let the Spirit of the Season have you.

DAY 346

Our Blessings

Nothing in this world is really ours. Even if we work for something, what we receive is not really a possession. It comes in, it goes out.

Everything we receive comes from the Divine.

Nothing belongs to us — our time, our love, our money, our creativity — yep, all from the Divine.
We are the receiver.

We are blessed in so many ways that we do not even recognize them.

Just for today...

... let the Spirit of All Your Daily Blessings have you.

DAY 347

First Day of Christmas

On the first day of Christmas my true love gave to me: a day of meditation, fasting and silence.

Just for today...

... let the Spirit of Deep Introspection have you.

DAY 348

Second Day of Christmas

On the second day of Christmas my true love gave to me: a day of choices; the freedom to consciously witness my decisions.

Just for today…

… let the Spirit of Your Choices have you.

DAY 349

Third Day of Christmas

On the third day of Christmas my true love gave to me: a day of plenty.

Just for today...

... let the Spirit of Enough have you.

DAY 350

Fourth Day of Christmas

On the fourth day of Christmas my true love gave to me: a day of chaos and tragedy. A day of cluttered thoughts, anger, helplessness. A day to remember that in chaos we can still feel safe; that in tragedy we can grieve together as a universal family.

In chaos we can still remember that in time all tragedy heals, that the meaning of such great loss to so many families will be revealed, that love is not loss and that the children who have left before us will help birth us when we leave this lifetime.

Just for today...

... let the Spirit of Divine Chaos and Tragedy have you.

DAY 351

Fifth Day of Christmas

On the fifth day of Christmas my true love gave to me:
a day of joy.

A day to be creative, to play, to pray — in equal balance, praying and playing.

Just for today...

... let the Spirit of Joy have you.

DAY 352

Sixth Day of Christmas

On the sixth day of Christmas my true love gave to me: a day of health.

A day to thank Spirit, through the energy of breath, for my healthy mind, body and spirit.

Just for today...

... let the Spirit of Health have you.

DAY 353

Seventh Day of Christmas

On the seventh day of Christmas my true love gave to me: a day of garbage.

A day to rummage through my ego and let go of old ideas, old habits, old thoughts.

Just for today...

... let the Spirit of Release have you.

DAY 354

Eighth Day of Christmas

On the eighth day of Christmas my true love gave to me: a day of darkness.

It is only in the darkest resources of my soul that I am able to rise again into light. The dark pushes me to be the best I can be.

Just for today…

… let the Spirit of Divine Darkness have you.

DAY 355

Ninth Day of Christmas

On the ninth day of Christmas my true love gave to me: a day of structure.

A day to start new habits, new rituals.

Just for today…

… let the Spirit of Structure have you.

DAY 356

Tenth Day of Christmas

On the tenth day of Christmas my true love gave to me: a day of happiness.

The physical world will only provide us with short-term happiness. When we create with the creator, we are filled with an inner happiness that is lasting inside and out.

Just for today...

... let Happy have you.

DAY 357

Eleventh Day of Christmas

On the eleventh day of Christmas my true love gave to me: a day of humility. A day to break through any barriers of my ego. A day to accept guidance. Sometimes we need to be broken to awake anew.

Just for today…

…let the Spirit of Humility have you.

DAY 358

Twelfth Day of Christmas

On the twelfth day of Christmas my true love gave to me: a day of service.

Be giving of your time, with no agenda. Give money that you've earned, to be of service, with no hidden agenda. Give until you feel like you can't take it anymore.

Just for today…

… let the Spirit of Service have you.

DAY 359

The Spirit of Christmas NOW

Christmas is a state of mind. If you believe, your mind will take you into a joy-filled state, no matter what your circumstances.

Gift-giving can be magical when you give unconditionally. What you give does not have to be a thing. Prayers and lighting candles are precious gifts to a receiver.

Try not to allow the confusion of the season cause you to hide or grumble.

Take what you need from it, but take with grace in mind and love in your heart.

This is a day and a season for remembering the love of a man who once lived on our planet and gave himself and his ideas freely.

Just for today...

... enjoy the Joy in Christmas.

DAY 360

The Spirit of the Season

May the Joy of the Season fill your hearts.
May any sadness fill you up to the awakening within.
Merry Christmas everyone, especially those no longer with us,
May their light shine brightly upon us as we continue our journey.

Just for today…

… let the Spirit of the Season have you.

DAY 361

The Spirit of Christmas

We collect and clutter

to own or give to another

but in the end,

it all gets lost — the paper, the trinkets, the glass.

But for now the gifting is sacred, the collecting a hobby,

so enjoy the moment, the season, the holly.

Just for today...

... let the Spirit of Giving have you.

DAY 362

The Spirit of Christmas Love

Snowballs, they are being thrown,
Lights, they are glowing,
Shopkeepers, they are grinning
Come on in, Come on in, Come on in.

It's the season of Joy
The Magic is in the eyes of every girl and boy
Grandmas are cooking and singing
Come on in, Come on in, Come on in.

There are those who have no one
They lost those they love and need someone
So today and for all days,
Let the Spirit of Love have you
Come on in, Come on in, Come on in.

Just for today…

… let the Spirit of Christmas Love have you.

DAY 363

The Spirit of Flow

What you resist will always persist.

Be like a river: allow the flow, stop wishing you were upstream.

Be where you are.

Let go; let flow.

Just for today…

…let the Spirit of Letting Go have you.

DAY 364

The Spirit of Loving Words

Words hold energy.

Energy is alive. When you gossip or speak ill of another, that energy is felt by the one spoken of. In the most subtle way you inflict pain or love. If you are speaking in the negative, you do not heal that person. Be careful with your words; they hold the energy to empower or disempower. Gossip is a thief; it takes more from the other than you can imagine.

Just for today…

… let the Spirit of Loving Words have you.

DAY 365

The Spirit of Sacred Activism

The past year is over and what have we done?
Did we give with gratitude or did we judge and give none.
As the new year approaches, opportunities have we
To help those in need; expect nothing in return please.
The whole world is crying, bleeding and dying
We can make a difference, so let us start trying.
Spiritual Warriors, Sacred Activists, let's set our intentions
To make this year different, without any question.

Just for today...

... let the Spirit of Sacred Activism have you and everyone.

About the Author

Lilly White was born on the Island of Newfoundland, Canada, the oldest of six children. She always believed in something bigger than herself. Being alone with angels and fairies was a rare gift that she embraced with love and affection for the unseen.

She and John, her husband of forty years, started a family when she was just eighteen. They raised two daughters and are now divine grandparents to six grandchildren — Breanna, Madeleine, Carter, Xavier, Tatiana, and Zofia.

John retired from thirty-five years with the Royal Canadian Mounted Police and travelled the world with the U.N. for seven years, so Lilly had the long-awaited opportunity to spend time alone and commune with the energies she longed for. During these years she opened a business called Whitelight and enjoyed many successful years working in marketing.

Later, while studying with Caroline Myss, it became clear to Lilly that it was going to be difficult to leave the monetary success of the marketing world, but Caroline said, "Oh, Lilly, you are just afraid to lose your STUFF." Lilly went home that week in 2006 and resigned from a job she loved because she realized that she was increasingly drawn to helping others fulfill their highest potential. She had lived her dream; now it was time to help others do the same – to help them jump off the cliff. She had jumped many times over the years, and had learned that no net is required. She had learned from experience to move from scarcity to an attitude of abundance.

Lilly began her personnel journey of enlightenment in 1991 when she entered a recovery program. Her years of study with experts such as Caroline Myss, Dr. Doreen Virtue, and Dr. Mario Martinez had prepared her for the plunge. Lilly and John moved to Almonte from Ottawa in December of 2006. She opened Whitelight Retreat to house The Trinity Table, an experiential medium for profound relaxation and spiritual and emotional healing, and to host personal development workshops.

In July of 2010 it became clear that Spirit had other plans for Whitelight Retreat. Its 1890 heritage home was sold to make room for Lilly's next adventure. Later that summer the house they were to purchase had a fire, which you'll read about in 2016 in *Lilly White Insights into Madnesss, Addiction & Love.* Not allowing losing a home to stop her, in April of 2011 she opened The White Lilly in Almonte, a retail/service business.

A year after the White Lilly opened, Lilly's daughter Melanie committed suicide, her mother died, and her dad had a stroke. Lilly closed the store in March of 2014 to make room for grief, and began to write daily inspirations for herself that evolved into *365 Ways to Power Up Your Life: Tools for Intuitive Living.*

Lilly visits Bali yearly and invites those interested to come along for the spiritual journey. If you would like to experience letting Spirit have you, Lilly will take you to Bali for your own spiritual journey during which she will help you understand the difference between fate and destiny. Spiritual journeys are usually in October or April each year, and are limited to four people so you can experience the depth and uniqueness of Bali and enjoy Lilly's spiritual family, Augung Prana.

Lilly is the creator of the monthly "Breakfast with Soul" gatherings and the biannual "Power Up Your Life" conferences, both held in Almonte, Ontario, and has hosted such visionaries as Andrew Harvey and Dr. Mona Lisa Shultz.

Lilly's vast knowledge, experience, and accreditations include:

Certified Sacred Contract Counsellor

Certified Medium

Certified Angel Therapy Practitioner and Medium

Reiki Master

Trinity Table Facilitator

Author of:

Lilly White Lies & Dreams

365 Ways to Power Up Your Life

Power Up Your Life 30-Day Challenge Workbook

and, to be released in 2016, *Lilly White Insights into Madness, Addiction & Love*

Lecturer

Spiritual Coach

Find out more at www.lillywhite.ca

www.ingramcontent.com/pod-product-compliance
Lightning Source LLC
Chambersburg PA
CBHW060235100426
42742CB00011B/1532

* 9 7 8 1 9 3 4 5 0 9 8 8 3 *